Read-Aloud Handbook

Grade 4

Table of Contents

Introduction 4

Unit 1: Government at Work
Essential Question: Why do we need a government?

Jake and Jackie for President 8
Government Is for Kids 10
John Muir: A Friend of Nature 12
Let's Celebrate! 14
What Is a Jury? 16

Unit 2: Characters Facing Challenges
Essential Question: What can we learn when we face problems?

Hadley, the Helped-Along Walrus 18
Princess Clarabelle 20
The Giving Dog, Part 1 22
The Giving Dog, Part 2 24
Silly Things 26

Unit 3: Plants and Animals in Their Habitats
Essential Question: How do living things get what they need to survive?

Worms to the Rescue 28
In the Garden 30
Fly Away, Ladybug! 32
Keeping Warm 34
I, Mouse 36

Unit 4: Many Characters, Many Points of View
Essential Question: How can a story change depending on who tells it?

Dog Talk 38
Dad's Big News 40
The Basket Weaver, Part 1 42
The Basket Weaver, Part 2 44
Good Sports 46

Unit 5: Solving Problems Through Technology
Essential Question: Where do ideas for inventions come from?

Are You Meant to Invent? 48
The Wright Brothers Take Off 50
Willy Wriggler's Wheels 52
Texting: Yes or No? 54
The Traffic Signal: A Bright Idea from a Bright Inventor 56

Unit 6: Tales to Live By
Essential Question: What can different cultures teach us?

A Man and His Precious Cow 58

Happy New Year!/Chinese New Year 60

Brother Tiger and the Well, Part 1 62

Brother Tiger and the Well, Part 2 64

Sijo Poems 66

Unit 7: Investigating the Past
Essential Question: How does understanding the past shape the future?

Long Gone 68

Dana Daring: Dino Detective 70

Next Stop, Mummies! 72

The Scoop on Dino Poop 74

Homes in the Cliffs 76

Unit 8: Wind and Water Change Earth
Essential Question: How do we react to changes in nature?

The Wind/Spring 78

Ten Thousand Buffalo on Our Roof 80

What Makes Wind? 82

Catching Snowflakes/Snow Birds 84

Where's the Water? 86

Unit 9: Buyers and Sellers
Essential Question: How do the goods we make, buy, and sell connect us?

Swap It! 88

The Little Lemons 90

What Is Art Worth? 92

The Potter's Wheel 94

The Gift 96

Unit 10: States of Matter
Essential Question: How can something old become new?

Turning Trash Into Art! 98

Temika Makes Paper, Part 1 100

Temika Makes Paper, Part 2 102

Our Stream Team 104

Mushy Bananas 106

Grade 2 Passage Matrix 108

Introduction

The Value of Reading Aloud to Students

Reading aloud to students is one of the best ways to engage them with the text. Students of all ages love to be read to, and as teachers read stories, poems, and informational texts to their students, they model the joy of reading and the range of genres and text types students will encounter in their own reading.

Interactive read-alouds serve the added purpose of providing teachers with opportunities to demonstrate thinking while reading a text to students. In the Benchmark Advance program, teachers are encouraged to use classic and contemporary read-alouds to model the metacognitive strategies all readers use.

Metacognitive strategies support readers to develop and deepen their comprehension of a text before, during, and after they read. Through the application of metacognitive strategies in the classroom, students think about thinking and develop as readers.

In the Benchmark Read-Aloud Handbook, the instruction supports teachers to model and guide practice with these strategies. From grade level to grade level, as well as throughout each grade level, students review previously taught metacognitive strategies and learn how to integrate them into their reading. Through instruction and practice, students can develop the ability to draw on multiple metacognitive strategies during every reading experience.

Supporting Common Core Standards Through Read-Alouds

The read-aloud selections and instruction in this handbook support a range of Common Core Standards. Teachers support students' foundational reading skills as they model reading prose and poetry with accuracy, appropriate rate, and expression. As students listen with purpose and understanding, paraphrase the texts, and discuss ideas with peers, they enhance their speaking and listening skills. The interactive read-aloud prompts also support students' ability to use text evidence to answer a range of text-dependent questions.

Using the Read-Alouds

Within the *Benchmark Advance* program, the Read-Aloud Handbook is listed in the Suggested Pacing Guide and in the Whole Group overview pages.

This handbook provides read-alouds for each of the 10 units in *Benchmark Advance*, Grade 2. You may use the read-alouds in any order you choose. Think of them as a resource to draw from to extend content knowledge beyond the selections in the Texts for Close Reading units.

Modeling the Metacognitive Strategies

As you use the Read-Aloud Handbook, you can guide instruction with the following model prompts.

Introduce the Passage

Read the title, share information about the author, invite students to share their ideas on what the passage is about, and engage students with additional information.

Explain the Strategy

Each unit's selections reinforce a specific metacognitive strategy. Explain to students that as you read, you will model the strategy. At least one of the interactive read-aloud prompts per selection supports the metacognitive strategy.

Read and Think Aloud

Read aloud the text with fluent expression. As you read, stop occasionally to think aloud and model the target metacognitive strategy. Use the sample prompts during reading to help you formulate think-alouds for the passages you are reading.

You may wish to write thoughts on self-stick notes and place the notes on the page as students watch. In order to keep students engaged, the Read-Aloud Handbook provides four think-alouds during the reading. More frequent interruptions may lead to confusion.

After Reading

You may ask questions to focus conversation on the habits of readers. For example:

• What did you see me do as I read the passage?

• What kinds of questions did you see me ask?

• What kinds of inferences did I make?

• Where did I find the important information?

• How did I summarize and synthesize information as I read? How did that help me?

• What information in the text helped me visualize?

• What did I do to "fix up" my comprehension?

Create a class Metacognitive Strategies Anchor Chart based on the information generated during your discussions in each unit. Save this anchor chart and add to it each day as you continue to focus on the same strategy.

Turn and Talk. Invite students to share examples of metacognitive strategies they used as they listened to the text. Ask partners to share their ideas with the whole group.

Connect and Transfer. Remind students that readers need to be active and engaged with the text whenever they read and that you would like them to consciously practice using this strategy until it feels natural and automatic.

Metacognitive Strategies At a Glance

Ask Questions	Readers ask questions before they read. They often pause during reading to ask questions that help them understand and stay involved in what they are reading. Readers sometimes ask questions after they read. Readers ask the following kinds of questions: • Questions about unfamiliar words or confusing information • Questions that have answers right in the text • Questions that have answers that can be inferred from the text • Questions that are not answered in the text and will need further research or discussion
Visualize	Readers visualize when they form pictures in their minds to help them "see" and understand characters, settings, objects, and actions they are reading about. Readers visualize by using the following kinds of information: • Vivid verbs that describe actions • Adjectives that describe size, shape, color, and other details • Graphic aids that tell size, shape, length, distance, time, and other information (such as charts, maps, time lines, diagrams, etc.) • Similes and metaphors that compare one thing to another • Sensory language that evokes how something feels, sounds, smells, or tastes
Determine Text Importance	Readers identify big ideas, themes, and specific information when they read. They may also evaluate the author's purpose and point of view. Readers determine text importance in the following ways: • Activate and build prior knowledge • Determine what is important versus what is interesting • Distinguish between what to read carefully and what to ignore • Highlight important words and nonfiction text features (captions, labels, bullets, etc.) • Make notes and drawings in the margin to understand and remember the text • Determine author's perspective, point of view, and/or opinion

Make Inferences and Predictions	Readers make inferences when they use clues and information in a text to figure something out that the author isn't directly telling them. Sometimes they also use their prior knowledge to help them. Readers make inferences by: • Using story clues to figure out what is happening or why it is happening • Using clues about characters (their actions, words, thoughts) to figure out what they are like and what they might do next • Using clues to figure out the book's themes, or "big ideas"
Summarize and Synthesize	Synthesizing is the opposite of analyzing. While analyzing requires readers to take text apart, synthesizing requires readers to put text together to form a new idea or perspective. Readers summarize and synthesize information in the following ways: • Summarize information by stating the big ideas • Make generalizations, judgments, and opinions • Distinguish between more important ideas and less important ideas • Stop to collect their thoughts about a topic before, during, and after reading
Make Connections	Readers make connections when they link what they are reading to something they already know. Readers make three types of connections to texts: • Text to self: the reader makes a personal connection with the text • Text to text: the reader makes a connection between the text he or she is reading and a text he or she has already read • Text to world: the reader makes a connection between the text and something in the world at large
Fix-Up Monitoring	When comprehension breaks down, readers use fix-up monitoring strategies to repair their comprehension. Some of the fix-up strategies readers use are: • Stop and reread to clarify meaning • Read ahead to clarify meaning • Talk about what is confusing in the text • Write about what is confusing in the text

Objective

• Model asking questions

Set the Stage

Introduce the Text *Today I'm going to read aloud a story called "Jake and Jackie for President." The main characters are twins, and they both want to run for school president! Jake is very friendly, and Jackie has great ideas.*

Engage Thinking *Which of the twins do you think would make a good school president, and why? Turn to a partner and share your prediction.*

Engage with the Text

Read aloud the text at a fluent, expressive pace. Use the suggested prompts to model your thinking, clarify events, and elicit student interaction.

1. *Turn and talk to a partner. Ask each other what "friendly" means and who is friendly in the story. Use complete sentences to answer the questions.* (Ask questions)

2. *Have students ask each other questions covering topics such as who they think should be class president, Jackie or Jake, and why. Use complete sentences to answer the questions.* (Ask questions)

Jake and Jackie for President

by J. McGillian

1   Jake and I had decided to run for school president a short time ago. Mom had suggested it to me while we were grocery shopping. She said, "Jackie, you've got such great ideas. You should run for school president."

2   Dad had suggested it to Jake while they were cooking dinner. Dad had said, "You know, Jake, with your friendly personality, you would make a great president. Why don't you run?"

3   When we got home from the store, Jake said, "Guess what?"

4   And I said, "Tell me after I tell you my big news."

5   Our announcements, that we were each planning to run, came out of our mouths at the same split second. That's twins for you.

5   First, I offered to drop out of the race. Then Jake said he would drop out.

6   Did we really want to run against each other?

7   But Jake told me that I definitely should run.

8   And I told Jake that he definitely should run. **2**

9   Every kid in the school likes Jake. He's friendly, outgoing, and he's definitely not shy. Jake is the kid who says hi to everyone, even the lunch ladies.

10 I am not that kid. I am the shy, quiet girl with good grades and a bookworm personality. But the thing is, what Jake has in personality, I have in ideas.

11 I want school to be full of learning and fun. I want a mid-year dance and I want Mr. Science to visit our classrooms. I also want an afterschool club, such as cooking or swimming.

12 We talked to Principal Green about how we both signed up to run for president without knowing that the other one was even running. Mr. Green said that one of us could be president and the other could be vice president. We both seemed to like that idea. Then he asked us which one would want to be vice president. Neither one of us wanted that.

13 So, just before voting time, Jake and I took the stage for our final speech. Actually, I wrote the words, and Jake recited them. Then he asked the students what they thought of us running together. He said, "Vote for Jake and Jackie and you will get two presidents in one. That's twice the fun." **3**

14 The crowd went wild.

15 The rest is history. **4**

3. *The narrator wrote the words in the speech, "… get two presidents in one. That's twice the fun." The rhyme makes it fun to say, and it supports the reason why the twins want to run together.* (Analyze the text)

4. *Turn and talk to a partner. Ask: Why did the twins decide to run together as one president?* (Summarize/Ask questions)

Extend Thinking Questions

Pose one or more questions to engage students more deeply with the text.

• *In this story, Jackie feels like she would be a good president for the school. How does she describe her personality, and what ideas does she have for making the school better?*

• *What would make you a good school president?*

iELD Paraphrase to Support Comprehension

After sentence 1: *Jake and the narrator, Jackie, wanted to be the student leader of their school.*

After paragraph 11: *Jackie is not like her brother, Jake. Instead, she reads a lot and doesn't go out of her way to say hello to people she barely knows. But Jackie thinks she has great ideas, just as she thinks Jake has a great personality.*

After paragraph 14: *Jackie writes the words in a speech for Jake to tell the students of the school. He explains that he and his sister, Jackie, will be running together as one school president.*

CCSS
RL.2.1, RL.2.3, RL.2.4, L.2.4c

Government Is for Kids

by Mike Weinstein

1 You know what? You are lucky to be hearing this! In the early 1900s, many American kids worked eight or more hours a day, six days a week. They couldn't go to school.

2 But some adults said that education is important. They thought all children should go to school. The federal government in Washington, D.C., agreed. It made full-time work by young children illegal, or against the law. **1**

3 Most people don't spend much time thinking about the federal government. After all, most of you don't often see government workers in your school or in your town. But the federal government is a powerful force in our country. When it makes rules, the whole country must obey them.

4 The government's work extends far beyond Washington, in ways that might surprise you.

5 Ever ride in a car? Of course you do! The government builds and maintains many highways and bridges. It makes laws about the safety of cars. Safety, in fact, is an important part of the government's work. For example, it makes sure that your toys are safe. Recently, some electric cars and trucks that kids can ride were catching on fire. The government found out about the fires and recalled the toys. (A recall means that the toy maker must fix the problem if customers return the toy to be fixed.) With an adult's help, you can report unsafe toys to the government on the Internet. **2**

6 Delivering the mail is one of the government's most important jobs. **3** The United States Postal Service brings you postcards from traveling friends and takes your thank-you notes to Grandma. Post offices are found in the biggest cities and the smallest villages. Every time you drop an envelope in that blue mailbox, you are using a government service.

7 Have you ever gone camping in a national park? Thank your federal government for making the campsite available. Did you watch Sesame Street when you were younger? Money from the government helped to pay for that program and the public broadcasting system that showed it.

8   The government has made important changes in our public schools. Long ago, in many places white students and black students were not allowed to go to the same public school. The government wanted schools to be fair to all. It made a rule that public schools were for all kids. Today the government pays for school lunches for some students. It also pays for special programs for students who need extra help. **4**

9   Washington, D.C., may be far away from your home and school. Even so, the federal government touches you almost every day of your life.

3. *I wonder why the author says that delivering mail is one of the government's most important jobs? And why are post offices found everywhere? Is it because it's a way to communicate and send things to people far away?* (Ask questions)

4. *Turn and talk to a partner. How has the government helped public schools and students?* (Summarize/synthesize)

Extend Thinking Questions

Pose one or more questions to engage students more deeply with the text.

• *In this text, the author says that safety is an important concern for the government. What are some examples of safety that the author mentioned?*

• *How do you think you would feel if you had to work all day instead of go to school?*

iELD Paraphrase to Support Comprehension

After paragraph 2: *Children used to work all day, almost every day, and they couldn't go to school. Grown-ups who work for the government changed the law so that kids could have the right to go to school.*

After paragraph 3: *Everybody who lives in a country has to follow the government's rules.*

After last paragraph: *The U.S. government does a lot for the nation. It helps people stay safe. It helps people communicate with each other by mail. It helps provide ways to have fun. It helps keep public schools fair to everyone.*

CCSS
RI.2.1, RI.2.4, L.2.4a, L.2.4b, SL.2.4

Objective
• Model asking questions

Set the Stage

Introduce the Text *Today I'm going to read aloud an article called "John Muir: A Friend of Nature." It is a true story that explains how a man named John Muir explored the United States in the 1800s and early 1900s, recognized its natural beauty, and worked to preserve it.*

Engage Thinking *How do you think John Muir worked to preserve the country's natural beauty? Turn to a partner to share your prediction.*

Engage with the Text

Read aloud the text at a fluent, expressive pace. Use the suggested prompts to model your thinking, clarify events, and elicit student interaction.

1. *"He wrote about the beautiful places" uses the past tense, "wrote," of an irregular verb, "write." And earlier in the paragraph, "sprung" is used as the past tense of the irregular verb, "spring."* (Use past tense of irregular verbs)

2. *The part of the sentence, "John Muir's writing helped teach people," uses an apostrophe-s in his last name, Muir. That is to show that John Muir is the one who did the writing. That makes his name a possessive noun, showing that he is the owner of his writing.* (Understand possessive nouns)

John Muir:
A Friend of Nature

1   America's cities are amazing centers of business and modern life. They show how busy our world can be. But what about the quiet beauty of nature? Where can someone go in the United States to understand how beautiful our country is? There is beauty all around us, in local parks and even in backyards. But some of the most amazing landscapes in the United States can be found in our national parks and state parks. These are places set aside by our government so that people cannot change them.

2   One man has become known as the "Father of National Parks." In the 1800s, cities and towns sprung up around the nation. That's when a smart and clever outdoorsman named John Muir had a great idea. He thought it was important to save and learn about some of the country's amazing outdoor places. The nature-lover from Wisconsin spent time traveling the country. He recorded the different plants and animals that he saw. He wrote about the beautiful places that he visited. **1**

3   Long ago, it was difficult for people to travel around the country a lot. It took a long time to get from place to place with horses. People did not zip around on vacations like they do today. This is why John Muir's writing helped teach people about how special the natural landscapes of the country are. His work helped the government set aside areas as national parks. **2**

4   In 1903, John Muir invited President Theodore Roosevelt on a camping trip. The men spent three nights in the Yosemite Valley. **3** The valley and the beautiful Sierra Nevada Mountains were all around them. The trip helped the president understand the importance of this great valley. Yosemite was not the first national park. But the camping trip brought the country's attention to the importance of nature. It helped people see that a strong country respects its natural beauty. John Muir's work helped the country understand that we must save beautiful outdoor places for future Americans to enjoy.

5   How has the government helped to save the natural beauty of your state? Do you know where national and state parks are located near you? **4**

The John Muir Memorial in Yosemite National Park

Theodore Roosevelt visiting Yosemite Valley, 1903

3. *I wonder why John Muir invited President Theodore Roosevelt to spend time with him in the mountains? How could his invitation to the U.S. president help keep the country beautiful?* (Ask questions)

4. *Turn and talk to a partner. Ask each other: How has the government helped to save the natural beauty of your state? Do you know where national and state parks are located near you?* (Ask questions)

Extend Thinking Questions

Pose one or more questions to engage students more deeply with the text.

- *What is John Muir's nickname and why was he called that?*

- *How can the government help with preserving the beauty of its country?*

iELD Paraphrase to Support Comprehension

After paragraph 1: *The United States government can make places in its country off limits for changing in order to preserve the natural beauty of the land.*

After paragraph 2: *John Muir traveled the country long ago and began taking notes of where the most special natural landscapes are located.*

After paragraph 4: *John Muir spent time camping with President Roosevelt in 1903 and showed him the importance of preserving some lands, such as Yosemite Valley in California.*

CCSS
RI.2.1, RI.2.4, L.2.1d, L.2.2c, SL.2.3

Set the Stage

Introduce the Text *Today I'm going to read aloud two letters that discuss the idea of having a town parade. A second grade class shares the people they would like to include and why these people help make the town great. The mayor responds in favor of the idea and explains the reason why their town has grown and stayed strong.*

Engage Thinking *What kinds of people are needed in order for a town to be strong? Turn to a partner to share your prediction of the people the class might want to include in the town parade.*

Engage with the Text

Read aloud the text at a fluent, expressive pace. Use the suggested prompts to model your thinking, clarify events, and elicit student interaction.

1. *I wonder why the class is so proud of the town. Is the town made up of special people?* (Ask questions)

2. *The words "children" and "people" are used in this paragraph. They are irregular plural nouns, because the singular nouns are "child" and "person." You have to do something else besides add an -s or -es to the end of these singular nouns to make them plural.* (Use irregular plural nouns)

Let's Celebrate!

1   Dear Mayor Bradley,

2   We have been learning in our classroom about the history of our town, Maple Grove. We know that the town is about to have its 150th birthday. We are so proud of this town! Do you think that we can have a parade to celebrate the town's birthday? **1**

3   A parade of the school children and local groups might be a great way to start the parade. Our school band can play the Happy Birthday song as we march. Then local groups can march, such as scout groups and people from the senior citizen's center. Then local businesses can march, too. We would also like to see some people from the police, fire fighters, and emergency medical groups marching in the parade. And we hope that you can be the first one in the parade line, Mayor Bradley! **2**

4   We know that it takes all of these groups and people to make a great town like Maple Grove. We want everyone to take part in the celebration. A town like ours is important, and our local government makes it a safe and fun place to live. That's why we want to ask you about planning a birthday event that we can all celebrate together.

5   We look forward to hearing from you soon about our idea.

Sincerely,

Mrs. Loo's 2nd Grade Class

1 Dear Mrs. Loo's 2nd Grade Class,

2 I was delighted to read your letter requesting a parade to celebrate Maple Grove's 150th birthday. I have been trying to think of the best way for the town to celebrate this happy day, and your idea is my favorite. It will be wonderful to get the townspeople together on this important day. **3**

3 I am always impressed with the way different parts of the town work together. You seem to understand, too, that working together is important for a local community. The police, school children, fire fighters, local businesses, and scout troops work with the rest of the town to make it a great place to live. I am always so proud to go to work each day as this town's mayor. Citizens like you make my job so enjoyable! **4**

4 I will work with you to plan the parade. As we celebrate our town, we must remember the reason Maple Grove was started 150 years ago. People wanted a safe place to live and raise their families. The town was started so there would be laws and a government to keep us safe. I am proud that the town has grown and stayed strong for so long.

5 I will be very happy to march in the parade with you.

Sincerely,

Mayor Anna Bradley

3. *"Townspeople" is a compound word that is made up of two individual words, "towns" and "people." So it must mean "people of the town."* (Determine word meaning)

4. *Turn and talk to a partner. Describe what makes the mayor's job so enjoyable.* (Summarize)

Extend Thinking Questions

Pose one or more questions to engage students more deeply with the text.

- *Who did Mrs. Loo's second grade class want to include in the parade to celebrate the town's birthday?*

- *According to Mayor Bradley, what purpose do the town's laws and government serve for its people?*

iELD Paraphrase to Support Comprehension

After paragraph 3, first letter: *A class wants to have a parade full of local groups and government workers, including the mayor of the town. They are writing the mayor to ask if she would allow the parade as a celebration of the town.*

After paragraph 4, response letter: *Mayor Bradley accepts the idea of having the parade to celebrate their town. She explains that the town was started 150 years ago with laws to keep the people safe.*

CCSS
RI.2.1, RI.2.4, L.2.1b, L.2.4d, SL.2.2, SL.2.3

Set the Stage

Introduce the Text *The U.S. government works to make sure that its citizens obey its laws. Many people work together for this goal, including a jury. These grown-ups listen to all of the facts before deciding if someone has or has not followed the laws. Today I'm going to read aloud an informative article that explains what a jury is.*

Engage Thinking *How would you describe what would make a good jury member?*

Engage with the Text

Read aloud the text at a fluent, expressive pace. Use the suggested prompts to model your thinking, clarify events, and elicit student interaction.

1. *The word "judge" has the /j/ sound in two places. Notice how the letter "j" and the letters "dg" make the same sound.* (**Learn spelling patterns**)

2. *This paragraph uses the collective nouns "jury" and "group." Both of these words describe the members as a whole.* (**Use collective nouns**)

What Is a Jury?

1   In the United States, people follow laws set up by the government. But how can we know for sure if someone has not followed a law? The police may ask a person to appear in a place called a court. A court is a building where people meet to decide if people have followed the law. People agree to go to the court and tell the truth about their story and what happened. A person called a lawyer will often help people to tell their story and to gather information that might show that they are telling the truth.

2   A judge is a person in charge of a court of law. The judge agrees to be fair and hear both sides of a story. Have you ever gotten into an argument with a friend? You might go to a parent or teacher to tell your story. The person who listens to both sides of the problem does the similar job of a judge. **1**

3   The other people in a court are called the jury. That's a group of people who also agree to listen to all of the details about a person's story. They decide together if a person has committed a crime. If there was a crime, the judge decides what the punishment will be. **2**

4   Being on a jury can be an interesting experience. The founders of the United States wanted to set up our court system so that regular, everyday citizens can take part in the law system. A jury is made up of average people in the local community. They take turns going to the court and listening to the details of a person's story. **3**

5 Juries take their jobs very seriously. They decide if a person has not followed the law. A jury's decision can cause someone to go to jail. Its decision can also keep someone from being sent to jail. The role of a jury is important. **4**

6 Imagine that you were accused of a crime, but you think you are innocent. You would want a good group of jurors to listen to your case. A jury will do the best they can to make sure they make a correct and fair decision.

3. *Have students ask each other questions about why the United States' founders wanted regular citizens to make up a jury. Have them use complete sentences to answer the questions.* (Ask questions)

4. *Turn and talk to a partner. Ask each other what it means to be on a jury. Use complete sentences to answer the question.* (Ask questions)

Extend Thinking Questions

Pose one or more questions to engage students more deeply with the text.

• *Why is it important for jury members to listen carefully to all of the details in court?*

• *How does the U.S. government deal with somebody who might have broken the law?*

Paraphrase to Support Comprehension

After paragraph 1: *The U.S. government uses a court of law to make sure that all people can tell their side of the story to find out the truth.*

After paragraph 5: *Members of a jury are needed to listen to facts and determine if someone has or has not obeyed the law.*

CCSS
RI.2.1, RI.2.4, L.2.1a, L.2.2d, SL.2.6

Objective

• Model visualizing

Set the Stage

Introduce the Text *Today I'm going to read aloud a fictional story about a walrus named Hadley. He had never felt quite at home in the zoo. This story starts at his first opportunity to travel elsewhere.*

Engage Thinking *What do you think will happen that will allow Hadley to travel elsewhere from the zoo? Turn to a partner to share your prediction.*

Engage with the Text

Read aloud the text at a fluent, expressive pace. Use the suggested prompts to model your thinking, clarify events, and elicit student interaction.

1. *The narrator uses the words "dug and dug" to describe how Hadley dug for a long time. The "pop!—up poked his bald head" helps me visualize his head with no hair quickly coming up from below.* **(Visualize)**

2. *The older woman says, "It's nice to find someone my own age." She thinks Hadley is an older person (because of his disguise and the way he wobbled). She thinks she has something in common with Hadley, and she likes that.* **(Use conversational phrases)**

Hadley, the Helped-Along Walrus

by Tim Bascom

1. Hadley the walrus knew that everyone at the zoo loved him—especially when he swam upside down. But no matter how hard he swam, Hadley never felt at home.

2. This pool couldn't be home. It was too small.

3. Then one day the zookeeper left his shovel nearby, so Hadley began to dig. He dug and dug until—pop!—up poked his bald head, right into the zoo bathroom. **1**

4. Could this be home?

5. No. Too smelly.

6. But someone had left a hat and raincoat, so Hadley put them on. He waddled outside.

7. "Come again," said the lady at the gate.

8. Hadley saw a bus on the street. "Step on up," said the driver.

9. "Sit here," said a little girl.

10. So Hadley did.

11. In the city, when everyone got off the bus, Hadley did, too. Stairs led down below the sidewalk to a saxophone player whose hat was full of money. Then came a bright screeching light and a whoosh of air.

12. Could this be home?

13. No. Too dark and loud.

14. The man with the saxophone spoke up. "Are you looking for the airport train? Just follow the crowd."

15. So Hadley followed. Doors closed behind him, and the train began to move. When everyone jumped out, so did Hadley.

16. Could this be home?

17. No. Too bright and busy.

18 But a man in a uniform was helpful. "Sir, you dropped your ticket! I see you're going to Alaska. You'd better hurry. Your flight is over there."

19 Hadley wobbled into a strange tunnel full of seats. A lady with high gray hair smiled. "It's nice to find someone my own age," she said. **2**

20 So Hadley sat beside her and looked out the window. He watched as trees rushed by, then clouds.

21 Could this be home? **3**

22 No. Too high and dry.

23 At least everyone was nice. "Have a good visit," said the flight attendant after they stopped moving.

24 "Need a ride?" asked his lady friend. "My son is picking me up and bringing the kids."

25 So Hadley rode along with his lap full of children. When everyone got out, so did he. Something smelled familiar—all salty and wet. He could hear waves slapping. Hadley leaned over the railing for a close look. So much water.

26 So deep and wide.

27 His friend with the gray hair seemed to understand. "Would you like a push?" she asked.

27 She helped him over the railing, and suddenly the world turned silent and blue. The water was so cool, so slick, that Hadley wriggled all over. Fish darted above him, like birds in the air. He could hear his heartbeat.

28 Hadley was home. **4**

© Benchmark Education Company, LLC

3. *This is the fourth time that "Could this be home?" has been used in the story. The fact that this line is repeated so many times must mean that it holds important meaning for the story. The walrus really wants to find his home.* (Determine text importance)

4. *Turn and talk to a partner. Describe how each place he went to couldn't be his home. What was too smelly? Too dark and loud? Too bright and busy? Too high and dry?* (Make connections)

Extend Thinking Questions

Pose one or more questions to engage students more deeply with the text.

• *What were the different modes of transportation that Hadley used?*

• *What was the first event that started Hadley on his journey?*

iELD Paraphrase to Support Comprehension

After paragraph 1: *Hadley the walrus didn't feel like he belonged.*

After paragraph 7: *Hadley wore human's clothing. So, the lady at the gate treated him like a person. She allowed him through the zoo's gate to the "outside" world.*

After paragraph 15: *Hadley followed the people off the bus. A train passed him and came to a stop. He followed the crowd of people. He got off with everybody else when it came to another stop.*

After paragraph 25: *The gray-haired woman from the airplane let Hadley ride in a car with her. Her son drove, and her grandchildren rode in Hadley's lap. When the car stopped, Hadley got out and heard the ocean waves.*

CCSS
RL.2.1, RL.2.3, RL.2.4, L.2.5a, L.2.6

Objective

• Model visualizing

Set the Stage

Introduce the Text *Today I'm going to read aloud a story about a young princess named Clarabelle. She wishes to do things that she thinks would make her happy, but her mother, the queen, continues to tell her that princesses are not supposed to do those things.*

Engage Thinking *What sort of things do you think Princess Clarabelle will want to do? Turn to a partner to share your prediction.*

Engage with the Text

Read aloud the text at a fluent, expressive pace. Use the suggested prompts to model your thinking, clarify events, and elicit student interaction.

1. *I can find out what a lute is by looking in a dictionary. It is an old stringed instrument similar to a guitar.* (Determine word meaning)

2. *Clarabelle pretended she was a leaping dolphin as she splashed and dunked in her bathtub. I can visualize water splashing around her tub as she dunks herself under the surface and comes out leaping like a dolphin.* (Visualize)

Princess Clarabelle

by Elizabeth Passarelli

1   *Being a princess is hard work*, thought Princess Clarabelle as she tried to sit up straight on her small and not very comfortable royal throne and watched a group of musicians play. Her mother and father, the king and queen, sat beside her and smiled politely as they listened to the lively tune.

2   Princess Clarabelle looked longingly at the big drum and wished she could play it. She tapped her foot to the beat. Her mother put a gentle hand on her knee to remind her that princesses don't tap their royal feet. Princess Clarabelle sighed.

3   When the music ended, Princess Clarabelle clapped along with the rest of the royal court. The musicians grinned broadly, and she grinned back.

4   "Clarabelle," her mother whispered in her ear, "princesses do not grin."

5   Clarabelle tried to smile politely, but a giggle bubbled up inside her and escaped. Her mother sighed.

6   That evening when the queen came to kiss her good night, Princess Clarabelle asked, "Mama, may I please learn to play an instrument?"

7   "Of course, my dear. I'll have the music master begin giving you lute lessons tomorrow," her mother answered. **❶**

8   "But Mama, I don't want to play the lute. I want to play the drums," Clarabelle said.

9   "Clarabelle, princesses don't play drums."

10   "Why not?"

11   "It's not princess-like," the queen said.

12   The next day, Princess Clarabelle and the queen took their daily walk in the royal garden. They admired all the royal roses and the royal lilies and the royal pansies. Clarabelle watched the royal gardener's children as they played ring-around-the-rosey until they all fell laughing on the grass. Clarabelle laughed, too, while the queen smiled. "Mama, let's play ring-around-the-rosey!" Clarabelle begged.

13   "Clarabelle, princesses don't fall on the grass," the queen answered gently. "I'm sorry."

14   "Princesses don't get to do anything," Clarabelle grumbled.

15 As she took her bath that evening, Clarabelle splashed and dunked in her royal bathtub, pretending to be a dolphin leaping. **2** She remembered the time she went with her mother and father to watch the royal ships come in. Clarabelle had seen people diving and swimming in the sparkling blue sea. She'd picked up a seashell and slipped it into her pocket to take home.

16 Once Clarabelle was in her royal nightgown, she opened her box of treasures and took out the seashell. She touched the shell's smooth inside and tried to peer into its spirals.

17 When the queen came in to kiss her goodnight, Clarabelle asked, "Mama, can I go swimming in the ocean?"

18 "Oh, Clarabelle," her mother answered.

19 "Princesses don't go swimming?"Clarabelle asked.

20 The queen shook her head. "I'm afraid not." Her eyes were sad. "I always wanted to swim, too." **3**

21 Clarabelle ran and got her shell from her box of treasures. She held it up to her mother's ear.

22 "Can you hear the sea?" she asked.

23 As the queen listened, her eyes grew wide with surprise. Then she laughed and gave Clarabelle a hug.

24 "Mama, what were you like when you were a princess?"

25 "Just like you, Clarabelle." Her mother smiled and kissed her good night.

26 The next morning, Princess Clarabelle was not in her royal bed. When the queen finally found her in the royal library, Clarabelle was searching the shelves.

27 "I can't find it," Clarabelle said.

28 "What are you looking for?" asked her mother.

29 "The book of rules for princesses," said Clarabelle.

30 "There is no book of rules, Clarabelle," the queen told her.

31 "Then where did they come from?" Clarabelle asked.

32 "I don't know," the queen said, thinking hard.

33 Clarabelle had an idea. "Why don't we write our own book of rules?" She grinned broadly.

34 The queen grinned back. "Why not?"

35 They sat down side by side at the royal desk and wrote rule number one: A princess may play the drums! **4**

---

3. *Turn and talk to a partner. What does the queen's response say about her own childhood?* (Make inferences)

4. *Princess Clarabelle wants to see for herself why she cannot do the things she wants to do, so she searches for a book of rules. When she finds that there isn't one, she decides to create her own so that she can do those things.* (Summarize)

Extend Thinking Questions

Pose one or more questions to engage students more deeply with the text.

• *What is the reason the queen did not allow her daughter to play drums?*

• *What other rules do you think will be included in the princess's new book of rules?*

iELD Paraphrase to Support Comprehension

After paragraph 2: *Princess Clarabelle really wanted to play the drum. When she tapped her foot to the music's beat, her mother did not allow it.*

After paragraph 7: *The queen would have given her daughter lute lessons. (A lute is an instrument with strings that plays softly.)*

After last paragraph: *The queen and Princess Clarabelle started writing their own book of rules for a princess. The rules would include being allowed to play the drums.*

CCSS
RL.2.1, RL.2.3, L.2.4e, SL.2.3

Objective
• Model visualizing

Set the Stage

Introduce the Text *Today I'm going to read aloud the first part of a story about a boy who has to give up a dog he helped to raise. While growing up in the care of the boy's family, the dog had been trained to assist people with special needs.*

Engage Thinking *How do you think the boy feels about giving up the dog? Turn to a partner to share your prediction.*

Engage with the Text

Read aloud the text at a fluent, expressive pace. Use the suggested prompts to model your thinking, clarify events, and elicit student interaction.

1. *I can visualize a happy puppy, wagging his tail and giving licks to the boy's smiling face.* (Visualize)

2. *At first I wasn't sure what "I have stood in your shoes" meant. But the next sentence is the boy asking her how she got through it. So "I have stood in your shoes" must mean "I have gone through this too."* (Determine word meaning)

The Giving Dog Part 1

by Jamie McGillian

1   Mrs. Regis was coming over to talk to me about Carson. Mrs. Regis is the woman in charge of an organization that matches people that have special needs with assist dogs. More than a year ago, my family volunteered to foster a puppy. We knew it wasn't permanent. Eventually, the puppy would have to leave to start his life of service. But it took just two licks and five wags to know that Carson would soon become my very best friend. **1**

2   I told myself that no one would ever separate us, but now that very thing was about to happen.

3   "I know this is hard, Danny," Mrs. Regis said, with her hand on my shoulder.

4   "I have stood in your shoes," she said. **2**

5   I asked Mrs. Regis how she got through it. She told me that her family focused on the good that they had done. I wasn't sure what Mrs. Regis was talking about. All I did was let a puppy into my life.

6   Then she told me that my family and I had done a very wonderful and responsible thing. Adopting a puppy while he is being trained as a service dog is very unselfish. **3** She reminded me that I taught Carson how to walk up the stairs. I remember Carson wanted nothing to do with it until I put a few treats on the top stairs. I was the one who took him out every morning and walked him for a half a mile. Even when I didn't want to get out of bed because Carson needed his exercise.

7   I was the one who groomed him and fed him, which helped him be a healthy dog. I didn't even know how to take care of myself, but I was able to take care of myself and Carson. That was something.

8   The first day I met Carson he was teeny-tiny and jittery. I held him for about fourteen hours. After that day, we were a team, and he never ignored me and always had time for me. **4**

3. *The word "unselfish" uses the prefix un-. I know that un- means "not," and "selfish" means "only caring about oneself." So "unselfish" means "not only caring about oneself," or "caring for others." (Determine word meaning)*

4. *Turn and talk to a partner. Describe what Danny remembered about helping Carson. How did this memory help Danny? (Summarize)*

Extend Thinking Questions

Pose one or more questions to engage students more deeply with the text.

• *Why is it so hard for Danny to say goodbye to Carson, the dog?*

• *Why did Danny feel better by realizing that he helped Carson?*

iELD Paraphrase to Support Comprehension

After paragraph 1: *A boy and his family had raised a puppy for more than a year. During that year, the puppy had been trained to help certain people. A woman came to take the dog to another person who needed the dog's help. But the boy didn't know how to say good-bye to his best friend, Carson the dog.*

After paragraph 4: *The woman understood how the boy, Danny, was feeling. She had been sad herself, from her own experience in the past.*

After paragraph 7: *Danny realized he had done a lot for the dog while it grew up.*

CCSS
RL.2.1, RL.2.3, L.2.3a, L.2.4b, SL.2.2

The Giving Dog, Part 2

Set the Stage

Introduce the Text *Today I'm going to read aloud the second part of "The Giving Dog," about the boy named Danny who has to give up the dog he helped raise. Let's recall what happened in Part 1.* (Have a volunteer summarize Part 1).

Engage Thinking *What emotions do you think the boy will feel toward the person who gets to live with Carson, the dog? Turn to a partner to share your prediction.*

Engage with the Text

Read aloud the text at a fluent, expressive pace. Use the suggested prompts to model your thinking, clarify events, and elicit student interaction.

1. *An adjective describes nouns or pronouns, while an adverb describes a verb, adjective, or other adverb. In the sentence that starts "He was born," "rare" and "eye" are adjectives that describe the noun "disease," while "almost" is an adverb that describes the adjective "blind."* (Use adjectives and adverbs)

2. *Danny describes what he did with Carson for the next two days. I can visualize the movies and pictures that were taken of them, and the treats and extra attention given to Carson as he left.* (Visualize)

3. *What things did Danny keep to remember the dog?* (Ask questions)

1 "You should be proud, Danny. You helped raise a puppy into a fine dog that is going to make a difference in someone's life."

2 Mrs. Regis handed me a small photograph of a little blond kid with an eye patch. At first, I thought she was showing me a picture of her son. Then she explained that the boy in the photo was Harry.

3 So that was the little squirt who was taking my puppy. I couldn't help but feel anger toward the kid.

4 Mrs. Regis went on to explain that Harry has had a difficult life. He's already had four operations on his eyes. He was born with a rare eye disease that has left him almost blind. **❶** If that wasn't bad enough, last year Harry's dad died. Harry lives with his mother and grandmother in a small house about three hours from here.

5 Mrs. Regis thinks that Harry and Carson would make an excellent team. Harry goes to a special school that allows guide dogs.

6 Carson at school? He would love that. Kids are Carson's favorite thing.

7 But Carson is leaving. I have to accept it.

8 For two days, I do nothing but make movies of Carson and take pictures of us. **❷** When Mrs. Regis comes to take Carson away, I send him off with a bag of treats, a picture of me, and half of his first blanket. I keep the other half of the blanket. **❸** Carson lets me slobber over him. Then he leaves with Mrs. Regis.

9 My parents tell me that I did a great job with Carson. Dad tells me that as soon as I'm ready, we can get another dog. I don't know how I feel about that. A week later I receive a letter.

10 Dear Danny,

11 I'm Harry and I think you've probably heard about me. At first, Carson was missing you a lot. I showed him your photo and he started barking. I know it must have been hard to say good-bye. I just want to say thank you for what you've given me.

12 From,

13 Harry

14 P.S. Feel free to write back.

15 I'm sure Harry and Carson are having fun right now.

4. *The letter uses a comma after the greeting (Dear Danny) and closing (From). This shows that there is a pause before the next line. (Reread ending to emphasize pause.) (Use commas in letters)*

Extend Thinking Questions

Pose one or more questions to engage students more deeply with the text.

• *Why did Harry write Danny? Do you think Danny is still angry with him for taking "his" dog?*

• *What are some good things that came from giving Carson to Harry?*

iELD Paraphrase to Support Comprehension

After paragraph 3: *A boy named Danny helped to raise a puppy to become a helpful dog. A woman came to take the dog to another person who needed the dog's help. She showed Danny a picture of the boy who would get to live with the dog. Danny felt angry with the boy for taking the dog from him, even though he had been expecting to have to say good-bye one day.*

After paragraph 4: *The boy who would be taking the dog has lived with many challenges already. The reason he needs the dog is to help him because the boy is almost blind.*

After P.S. of letter: *The new owner of Carson wrote a letter to Danny to say thank you for giving up the dog to help him. He also let Danny know that he could write him back.*

CCSS
RL.2.1, RL.2.3, L.2.1e, L.2.2b

Unit 2

Silly Things

by Alison Acheson

1 Dez counted. And counted again. Twenty-one red paper hearts he'd cut out for his kindergarten class. He counted the class list again. Very carefully.

2 "Slow down," his teacher had told him just yesterday at school. "Take your time."

3 Twenty-two. He needed twenty-two paper hearts.

4 "Your face is long." Mom spoke from the kitchen doorway.

5 "There's no paper left, and I need one more heart," Dez told her. "Can we go to the store again?"

6 Mom went away but came back with his jacket. "We have just enough time before the store closes," she said. "If we hurry."

7 She probably added that last bit because Dez wasn't moving. He was counting his list CAREFULLY. Still twenty-two names. And still just twenty-one hearts. Then he put on his jacket.

8 "You tell me to hurry, and Mr. Donaldson tells me to slow down," he said as Mom backed the car out of the driveway and started down the street. "That's like trying to ride my bike backwards and forwards at the same time!" **1**

9 His mom laughed. "Trying to ride in two different directions," she said, "that would be pretty silly!"

10 "I do a lot of silly things lately," said Dez.

11 "You do?"

12 "Yep. Like not realizing I've finished my Popsicle and biting the wooden stick part." **2**

13 "Ouch!" said Mom. She stopped the car and waited for a pedestrian to cross at the light.

14 "Last week I checked out a library book," said Dez as they rounded the next corner. "And when I got back to my classroom, I realized I'd already read it. And yesterday, I tried to put my jacket on upside down with a big twist in the back!" **3**

15 "That must have been when Mr. Donaldson told you to slow down," Mom guessed.

16 Dez nodded.

17 Mom stopped the car. Dez undid his seat belt, but Mom didn't move. "What's wrong?" he asked her.

18 "You know what?" she said. "I can't remember why we're here!" Her forehead was all wrinkled up, and she looked sort of embarrassed.

19 "I need one more paper heart," Dez reminded her. They looked at each other and began to laugh.

20 "Now I've done a silly thing!" said Mom, and they were still laughing when they came out of the store with the thick red paper in a roll under Dez's arm.

21 Back home, Dez cut out the last heart and added it to the pile. Then slowly—one heart at a time—he wrote the names of his classmates. S-U-Z-A-N-N-E and S-E-A-N and G-R-I-F-F and all the others. But there was one heart left. It couldn't be!

22 "Another long face," said Mom as she placed two bowls of minestrone soup on the table.

23 "I did another silly thing." Dez showed her the heart. "We went all the way to the store and we didn't need to. I counted wrong."

24 How could it be?

25 He read his list again and put a check mark by each name he'd printed. There was a card for everyone in his class.

26 No, not quite everyone. There was one person he'd forgotten. One person who sometimes did silly things.

27 A smile spread across his face, and he reached for the last red paper heart. With the big thick purple felt pen he printed D-E-Z.

28 Happy Valentine's Day, Dez! **4**

3. *"Last week I checked out a library book"* could be rewritten to have the same meaning. For example, Dez could have said, *"I checked out a library book last week."* Or he could have said, *"A library book was checked out by me last week."* (Rearrange sentences)

4. *Turn and talk to a partner. Retell the story, and be sure to include all of the silly things that happened.* (Summarize)

Extend Thinking Questions

Pose one or more questions to engage students more deeply with the text.

• *How did Dez respond when he realized he had made a card for himself?*

• *Mr. Donaldson tells Dez to slow down. What is the point of going slowly? Can you think of a time when you did something too quickly?*

iELD **Paraphrase to Support Comprehension**

After paragraph 4: *Dez had 21 hearts, but he needed one more for all the kids in his class. His mom told him, "Your face is long," which is a way of saying, "You look sad."*

After last paragraph: *Dez realized he had been counting his own name as part of the class list. So he ended up making himself a heart card, too!*

CCSS
RL.2.1, RL.2.3, L.2.1f, L.2.2a, SL.2.4

Objective

• Model determining text importance

Set the Stage

Introduce the Text *Today I'm going to read aloud an informational article about how worms and plants work together to help each other survive.*

Engage Thinking *How do you think plants use worms to survive? Turn to a partner to share your prediction.*

Engage with the Text

Read aloud the text at a fluent, expressive pace. Use the suggested prompts to model your thinking, clarify positions, and elicit student interaction.

1. *An adjective describes nouns or pronouns, while an adverb describes a verb, adjective, or other adverb. In the phrase "hard, dry dirt," "hard" and "dry" are adjectives that describe the noun "dirt." At the end of the sentence, "tightly" is an adverb that describes the verb "held."* **(Use adjectives and adverbs)**

2. *The phrase "lots of tunnels" is repeated. This emphasizes the important work that worms do for the plants.* **(Determine text importance)**

Worms to the Rescue

by Joy Elizabeth Hancock

1 The sunflowers were thirsty, but water ran off the dirt without soaking down to their roots. The sunflowers were hungry for more than sunshine, but there was nothing else. And the hard, dry dirt held the roots too tightly. **1** If the sunflowers could talk, they would have said, "Help!"

2 Those sunflowers needed earthworms to rescue them! Creepy, crawly, squiggly worms slowly tunnel their way through the dirt. With lots of tunnels here and lots of tunnels there, the dirt loosens up. **2** For plants this loose earth is sort of like a comfy blanket. Water can soak into loose dirt, and plants can drink the water. Roots can grow more easily. Plants and worms help each other. Worms eat dead leaves that fall off the plants. Then the worms poop out castings that the plants can eat.

3 Plants like lots and lots of worms. The more worms, the better! In one backyard, there can be thousands of hidden worms. Worms stay underground because they like to be cool and moist. Sometimes they will come up to the surface when it is dark and cool or rainy. But if the worms can't go back underground after a rain, they may dry out.

4 When worms dry out, they can't breathe and may die. You could easily rescue worms you find. Carefully take them to damp dirt where they can crawl underground. If you put worms in the dirt by your favorite flowers, the flowers will be happier. The worms will rescue your flowers, just as you rescued the worms! **3** **4**

3. *Turn and talk to a partner. Ask each other any questions you might have about how worms help plants, and try to answer them based on what we have read so far.* (Ask questions/ Summarize)

4. *This article is about the importance of worms and plants to each other. It even tells us how we can save worms from drying out and dying.* (Determine text importance)

Extend Thinking Questions

Pose one or more questions to engage students more deeply with the text.

• *Where do worms spend most of their time? Why?*

• *Plants and worms don't harm each other, but instead they help each other live and grow. Can you think of other living things that use each other to survive?*

iELD Paraphrase to Support Comprehension

After paragraph 1: *Dirt that is too packed is not good for plants.*

After paragraph 2: *Worms help loosen the soil by creating tunnels. Roots can then grow and easily soak up water. Worms eat plants' fallen leaves.*

After paragraph 3: *Worms live underground. They need to stay cool and moist.*

After paragraph 4: *Just as you can help worms, worms can also help flowers.*

CCSS
RI.2.1, RI.2.6, L.2.1e, SL.2.3

Set the Stage

Introduce the Text *Today I'm going to read aloud a poem written in the 1800s by a famous poet, Emily Dickinson. She describes what she sees as she watches a bird coming down a path.*

Engage Thinking *What do you think the bird will do? Turn to a partner to share your prediction.*

Engage with the Text

Read aloud the text at a fluent, expressive pace. Use the suggested prompts to model your thinking, clarify events, and elicit student interaction.

1. *This poem uses the rhythm of an ABCB rhyme scheme. This means that the last word of the second line rhymes with the last word of the fourth line: "saw" rhymes with "raw."* (Determine rhyme scheme)

2. *The author uses the verb "hopped" to describe how the bird went to the wall. If the author had used "stepped" instead, it would have described the human movement of just moving legs. If "jumped" had been used, it would have had more of an energetic movement—maybe like a frog or another animal.* (Model word choice)

3. *Turn and talk to a partner. Use complete sentences to explain what the author has noticed so far by watching the bird.* (Summarize)

In the Garden

by Emily Dickinson

A bird came down the walk:

He did not know I saw;

He bit an angle-worm in halves

And ate the fellow, raw. **1**

5   And then he drank a dew

From a convenient grass,

And then hopped sidewise to the wall **2**

To let a beetle pass.

He glanced with rapid eyes

10   That hurried all abroad, --

They looked like frightened beads, I thought; **3**

He stirred his velvet head

Like one in danger; cautious,

I offered him a crumb,

15   And he unrolled his feathers

And rowed him softer home

Than oars divide the ocean,

Too silver for a seam,

Or butterflies, off banks of noon,

20   Leap, plashless, as they swim. **4**

4. *This poem describes the natural behavior of a bird. It shows how it eats worms and drinks water, lets beetles pass, looks out for danger, and flies with grace.* (Determine text importance)

Extend Thinking Questions

Pose one or more questions to engage students more deeply with the text.

• *Why do you think the bird didn't take the crumb?*

• *How would you describe the bird in this poem?*

iELD Paraphrase to Support Comprehension

After stanza 1: *Someone watched a bird on a walkway. It did not see the person. The bird ate a worm.*

After stanza 2: *The bird drank drops of water from the dew of grass. A beetle walked by it.*

After stanza 3: *The bird looked around as if it expected danger. It shook its head.*

After stanza 4: *The person watching the bird offered it a crumb. The bird flew off.*

After stanza 5: *The bird flew gracefully as if it were swimming without splashing.*

CCSS
RL.2.1, RL.2.4, RL.2.6, L.2.5b, SL.2.4

Objective

- Model determining text importance

Set the Stage

Introduce the Text *Today I'm going to read aloud an informational text about the habits of ladybugs.*

Engage Thinking *If ladybugs need to stay warm, where do you think they like to sleep? Turn to a partner to share your prediction.*

Engage with the Text

Read aloud the text at a fluent, expressive pace. Use the suggested prompts to model your thinking, clarify positions, and elicit student interaction.

1. *This article starts off by telling us how long ladybugs live, and it explains how important it is for the bugs to find a warm spot to spend the winter. Let's read further to find out how ladybugs survive.* (Determine text importance)

2. *"Juicy" is an adjective that describes the aphids that ladybugs eat. It means aphids are full of juice. It makes me think of other things that are juicy that I eat, such as oranges, grapefruit, and watermelon.* (Make connections)

Fly Away, Ladybug!

1   Ladybugs or ladybird beetles can live for more than a year, so it's important for them to find a warm place to spend the winter. Most ladybugs will "overwinter" in cracks or crevices under rocks, near the bottom of fence posts, or under rotten logs. **❶**

2   Ladybugs do not eat or move all winter. This is their time to rest or hibernate. They live off the fat stored in their bodies from eating juicy aphids all summer long. **❷**

3   Some ladybugs in California will fly by the thousands in large red clouds to the Sierra Nevada Mountains. So many ladybugs swarm to the same spots each year that ladybug farmers collect the sleepy beetles to sell to gardeners in the spring. There can be as many as forty million ladybugs huddled in one pile! **❸**

4   Another favorite spot for ladybugs to keep warm is inside people's homes. On sunny fall days, swarms of ladybugs can climb the south side of a house to soak up the heat. Once on the house, ladybugs can crawl through the tiniest cracks under windows, siding, and roofing tiles.

5   If you find a ladybug in your house, don't worry. They are harmless and will not eat your food, plants, or clothing. Many people around the world even believe that having a ladybug inside the house is a sign of good luck. **❹**

3. *Let's use context clues in the sentence to figure out what "huddled" means. It is a verb that describes what the ladybugs are doing in the pile. If there are that many ladybugs in one place, it would make sense for "huddled" to mean "crowding close together."* (Determine word meaning)

4. *Turn and talk to a partner. Ask questions about what the ladybugs are doing in your home if it's not to eat.* (Summarize/Ask questions)

Extend Thinking Questions

Pose one or more questions to engage students more deeply with the text.

• *Where are some good places for ladybugs to hibernate all winter in nature?*

• *Where would be a safe, warm spot for a ladybug in your home?*

After paragraph 2: *A ladybug can live for more than a year. It needs a safe, warm spot to sleep all winter.*

After paragraph 5: *A ladybug might seek shelter in your home. It is so small that it can slip through cracks. It is not anything to worry about; it is just trying to get warm.*

CCSS
RI.2.1, RI.2.4, RI.2.6, L.2.4a, L.2.5a, SL.2.3

Unit 3

Set the Stage

Introduce the Text *Today I'm going to read aloud an informational text about the outer layers of various animals and how each animal is perfectly suited with its warm coat.*

Engage Thinking *What are some materials that act as coats for animals? Turn to a partner to share what you know.*

Engage with the Text

Read aloud the text at a fluent, expressive pace. Use the suggested prompts to model your thinking, clarify events, and elicit student interaction.

1. *An adjective describes nouns or pronouns. An adverb describes a verb, adjective, or other adverb, and many times ends in -ly. In the phrase "wonderfully warm, soft, downy feathers," "wonderfully" is an adverb that describes the following adjectives. "Warm, soft, downy" are the adjectives that describe the noun "feathers."* (Use adjectives and adverbs)

2. *"Feet" is an irregular plural noun. It is plural because there is more than one foot, and it is irregular because you have to do something other than add an -s or -es to the end of "foot" to make it plural.* (Use irregular plural nouns)

Keeping Warm

1 Human beings put on hats and coats and mittens when the weather gets cold. Animals have their own ways of staying warm.

2 Penguins have soft, downy feathers next to their bodies and dense, waterproof feathers covering the down. Emperor penguins keep their chicks warm and protected by tucking them under a flap of skin called a brood pouch. Groups of penguins huddle together against the cold and wind. Each penguin takes a turn standing on the outside while the other penguins get warm on the inside of the huddle.

3 Eider ducks have wonderfully warm, soft, downy feathers underneath their outer feathers. **1** Mother eider ducks pluck the down from their own breasts to line their nests. A bird's outer feathers are hollow. The air inside the feathers holds in body heat and helps keep the bird warm in cold weather. These outer feathers are layered like the tiles on a roof. They make a waterproof covering for the downy feathers underneath.

4 Ptarmigans have brown feathers in summer and then grow thicker, warmer, white feathers in winter. Unlike most birds, ptarmigans also have feathers that completely cover their feet. These feathers help the birds stay warm and keep their feet from freezing to the ice. **2**

5 Caribou grow thick, warm, waterproof coats in Arctic winters. Their broad feet are fringed with fur and keep the caribou from sinking into the snow. Caribou, Arctic foxes, and polar bears have thick fur coats. These coats are made up of lots and lots of individual hairs. Each hair has hollow spaces that are filled with air. This air traps the animal's body heat and helps keep the animal warm. **3**

6   Polar bears keep warm with two thick coats of fur. The outer coat of long, oily fur helps protect the soft, woolly undercoat next to the bear's skin. Under the skin is another warm layer, but it's made of fat not fur. This fat, called blubber, can be four inches thick and helps hold in the bear's body heat. The fur and blubber work so well that polar bears can actually get too hot and will stretch out on the ice to cool off.

7   In winter, Arctic foxes grow dense, white fur coats. They also have hair under their paws, to keep them warm and help them walk on top of the snow. **4**

---

3. *What is the purpose of hair that has hollow spaces? (Ask questions)*

4. *Turn and talk to a partner. The information in this text has explained how the feathers or fur of certain animals helps them stay warm. Their body heat helps them survive in cold climates. (Determine text importance)*

Extend Thinking Questions

Pose one or more questions to engage students more deeply with the text.

• *Why is it important that feathers are waterproof?*

• *Compare the feathered ptarmigan to the furry Arctic fox. How are they similar?*

Paraphrase to Support Comprehension

After paragraph 4: *Penguins and eider ducks have soft, downy feathers with waterproof feathers on top. This helps them stay warm in the cold climate. Penguins also stand close to each other to stay warm. Eider ducks make nests using their own feathers because they give such warmth. Outer feathers are hollow, so they hold in body heat. Ptarmigans have feathers that cover their feet. This keeps their feet from freezing on ice.*

After paragraph 7: *Caribou and Arctic foxes have furry feet to help them walk on snow. They have fur coats with hollow spaces in hairs that trap body heat. This helps keep them warm in the cold climate. Polar bears have three layers of warming protection: blubber (fat), a wool-like coat, and a long fur coat.*

CCSS
RI.2.1, RI.2.4, RI.2.6, RI.2.8, L.2.1b, L.2.1e

Set the Stage

Introduce the Text *Today I'm going to read aloud a poem. It is written from a mouse's point of view. It is a brave little mouse that narrates all of the fun it has in one night, while the people sleep.*

Engage Thinking *What do you envision the mouse doing at night while people sleep? Turn to a partner to share your prediction.*

Engage with the Text

Read aloud the text at a fluent, expressive pace. Use the suggested prompts to model your thinking, clarify events, and elicit student interaction.

1. *I want to check the spelling of "alley cat," so I will use a dictionary. I see that it is in the dictionary, between "alley" and "alley-oop." The dictionary tells me that "alley cat" is a homeless cat, so I know that the spelling is correct.* (Check spelling)

2. *The mouse is challenging the owl to chase it when it says, "I, Mouse, thumb my nose at night-hunting Owl." The informal phrase "thumb my nose" is a short way of calling the teasing action where you put your thumb on your nose and wiggle your fingers.* (Compare formal/informal English)

I, Mouse

You may think of me only as a small and timid mouse,
curled up in my soft bed of people socks,
but I, Mouse, have a secret.

At night, while the people sleep,
5   and the cat is nowhere to be seen,
I leave my hoard of seeds
and scurry up the back stairs.

I squeeze through a crack under the window,
climb onto the tree,
10 snap off the largest leaf,
and leap out into the windy, huge darkness.

I speed straight down to the people's high diving board
and perform a perfect swan dive into the pool.
The water is colder than an ice cube,
15 but it's not too cold for a tough skinny-dipping mouse like me.

After all that exercise, I'm hungry as an alley cat. **❶**
So I shake myself dry, sneak under the fence,
and steal the neighbor's biggest strawberry.
I get dizzy, it tastes so sweet.

20 I, Mouse, thumb my nose at night-hunting Owl. **❷**
I even tease her with a squeak.
And when Owl swoops over ready to pounce,
I run so fast
and hide so well,
25 she can never find me.

Some nights, the wind grows stronger.
My whiskers twitch at the wet smell in the air.
But the sudden lightning doesn't scare me.
I roar back at the thunder
30 louder than the thunder roars back at me.

And when the storm has passed,
and the great blackness of the sky
fills with a million shining seeds of light,
I stretch my paws wide
35 and spin and twirl
in a fantastical dance to the night.

Then, just before dark fades into day,
after one more whirl,
I scamper back up the tree,
40 squeeze under the window,
run down the stairs,
and slip into my cozy, warm hole in the wall.

So now you know that I'm not just a timid mouse
hiding away in a soft bed of people socks. **3**

45 I, Mouse, am a wild and daring mouse.
And I am depending on you, my friend,
to never tell anyone else my secret. **4**

3. *The details in this story have opened my eyes to the possible adventures that a mouse can have throughout the night while nobody is looking. Mice are sometimes known for being scared little creatures, but maybe they're braver than we think.* (Determine text importance)

4. *Turn and talk to a partner. What are the repeated words throughout this story, and what makes them so important?* (Determine text importance)

Extend Thinking Questions

Pose one or more questions to engage students more deeply with the text.

• *What chances does the mouse takes?*

• *What are your adventures that the mouse might find fun?*

iELD Paraphrase to Support Comprehension

After stanza 2: *You might think Mouse is easily frightened. But it secretly leaves its hiding place at night.*

After stanza 3: *It sneaks through a window. It rides on a leaf.*

After stanza 6: *It dives into a cold pool. But Mouse denies how cold it is. Mouse eats a strawberry. Then it challenges Owl to chase it. Mouse runs fast and hides.*

After stanza 8: *Mouse is not scared of lightning. It dances and spins after the thunderstorm ends.*

After stanza 11: *Mouse squeezes back through the open window. It goes back to its hiding place.*

CCSS
RL.2.1, RL.2.4, RL.2.6, L.2.2e, L.2.3a

Objective

• Model making inferences/predictions

Set the Stage

Introduce the Text *Today I'm going to read aloud a story, written from a dog's point of view. The dog tells us some tips for understanding "dog talk."*

Engage Thinking *What is the first thing you should do when you meet a dog if you want to pet it?*

Engage with the Text

Read aloud the text at a fluent, expressive pace. Use the suggested prompts to model your thinking, clarify events, and elicit student interaction.

1. *The word "probably" is an adverb meaning likely to happen. An adverb modifies a word or phrase. So, when we hear that "She'll probably say yes" in the text, we understand that "She will likely say yes."* (Use adverbs)

2. *There are three words that use contractions in this sentence: I'm, that's, and it's. Apostrophe -m stands for "am," and apostrophe -s stands for "is" in this context. So without the contractions, the words would be "I am," "that is," and "it is."* (Use apostrophes)

3. *Jake hopes the person in the shoes is a friend of his owner because he wants to be friendly. He does not want to have to protect his owner from harm; plus, he is so old, he may not be able to do much of anything anymore besides lie down and receive pats of love from a friend.* (Make inferences/predictions)

Dog Talk

by Pat Trollinger

1   Sniff, sniff.

2   Hello, Human. You say you like dogs? Want to learn a few secrets of Dog Talk? O.K., let's get started.

3   When I'm out for a walk, and we happen to meet, ask my human if it's O.K. to touch me. She'll probably say yes, and the first thing I'll want is a quick little sniff of your hand. **1**

4   Sniff, sniff. Are you nice?

5   Sniff, sniff. Gentle touch?

6   Sniff, sniff. Hey, you smell like a friendly person.

7   If my nose likes your scent and I'm eager for more, that's the signal— it's the right time to pet me. **2**

8   My neighbor, Bea, is so tiny and shy that she gets nervous the first time she sees you.

9   Arf, arf. You look tall!

10 Scamper, slide. Should I hide?

11 Oh, I'm glad that my human can hold me.

12 After Bea gets all snug in her owner's arms, she'll be calm while you tickle her ears.

13 My buddy, Jake, is getting old. Can you see the gray hair on his muzzle? His eyes aren't too strong, so he sniffs extra hard. He's had years of experience with Dog Talk.

14 Snuffle, sniff. I smell shoes.

15 Sniffle, whuff. Who are you?

16 I hope you are a friend of my human.

17 Old Jake will keep sniffling, and his owner will tell you if it's O.K. to pat his gray shoulders. **3**

18 Down the block, that's Rex. He's the grumpy type, and he usually hates any talking.

19 Bark, bark. Go away. This yard is all mine!

20 Grrr. Growl. I'm the world's greatest watchdog.

21 Let Rex do his job—stay away from his yard. His growling can get even louder.

22 Look at Lila, the puppy. She's all silly and soft, and she's not very good at sniffing.

23 Lick, lick. Feel my tongue. Nip, nip. Oooh, my teeth are really terrific!

24 That Lila is cute, but I hope she soon learns that a sniff is a better hello.

25 Hey, Human, please stay! This has been so much fun. Stick around, and I'll teach you more Dog Talk.

26 Sniff, sniff. Want to play?

27 Sniff, sniff. Got a ball?

28 Sniff, sniff. Say, do you have a treat in your pocket?

4. *Turn and talk to a partner. Ask each other and answer: Why do you think "Sniff, sniff" is written so often in this dog's story?* (Ask questions)

Extend Thinking Questions

Pose one or more questions to engage students more deeply with the text.

- *According to the narrator, what are the characteristics of the "world's greatest watchdog?"*

- *What does this selection tell you about how dogs like to be treated?*

iELD Paraphrase to Support Comprehension

After paragraph 7: *A dog gives tips on how to speak its language. Ask a dog's owner before you pet it. Let the dog smell you first.*

After paragraph 12: *Bea is a small dog that gets worried that she will get hurt. She barks and finds safety in the arms of her owner.*

After paragraph 15: *The narrator's dog friend, Jake, is old. It is hard for him to see you and smell you.*

After last paragraph: *Rex the dog barks and growls at people. He is not friendly, so stay away. Lila the puppy is soft and playful. The narrator loves chatting about dogs. But it also wants to play! And it would definitely eat a treat if you have one!*

CCSS
RL.2.1, RL.2.4, L.2.2c, L.2.1e

Unit 4

Dad's Big News

1 Mr. Johns pulled up to the house and ran up to the door. "Keisha, Jamar, come quick! I've got amazing news."

2 Jamar looked up from his math notebook. Keisha paused as she was teaching the new family puppy, Marcus, to roll over. "What is it?" said Keisha curiously.

3 "We're going on a vacation! I have to go on a business trip near Adventure World, and I'm allowed to bring my family for an extended weekend! Isn't that great? I just called your mom at work. We leave on Wednesday." **1**

4 Jamar jumped to his feet. "I can miss school for a few days!"

5 Mr. Johns shot Jamar a sly look. "Well, that is true, Jamar," he said. "But you will be making up all of the work you miss. You can't get away with not doing your schoolwork."

6 "Dad, I'm so excited," he said. "This is awesome! You know we've always wanted to go to Adventure World."

7 Keisha sat quietly, hugging Marcus close to her and stroking his long, white coat. "How could you do this?" Keisha said, holding back tears. "We can't leave Marcus alone or with a stranger. He's too young. He needs us." **2**

8 Mr. Johns' shoulders dropped and the smile quickly wiped from his face. "Oh, Keisha," he replied. "I thought you would be so happy. I think Marcus will be just fine at Grandma's house when we're gone. I know he's young, but he's always up for an adventure, right?" **3**

9 A tear rolled down Keisha's face. "I'll be thinking about him the whole time and worrying about him," she said. "He's our brand new puppy. How could we leave him so soon?"

10 Feeling sorry for his sister, Jamar spoke up. "I'll miss Marcus, too," he said. "But maybe we can start bringing him to Grandma's now so he can get used to it. And when we're there, I can teach Grandma how to text photos from her cell phone so she can let us know every day what Marcus is up to and how they are doing."

11 "Great idea," said Mr. Johns. "I think she'll get the hang of using some technology to keep us in touch with our pup, don't you think, Keisha?" **4**

12 Keisha smiled. "Yeah, maybe that's not a bad idea," she said looking at Marcus as he wagged his tail and panted happily. "Maybe going to Adventure World isn't such bad news after all."

Unit 4

3. *Mr. Johns says the dog is "always up for an adventure." That is an informal way of saying it is always ready to have fun and try new things. (Compare formal/informal English)*

4. *Turn and talk to a partner. Do you think Keisha has changed her mind about going to Adventure World? Why or why not? (Make inferences/predictions)*

Extend Thinking Questions

Pose one or more questions to engage students more deeply with the text.

• *Why was going on a vacation bad news according to Keisha?*

• *What was Jamar's plan that turned Keisha's sad tears into a smile?*

iELD Paraphrase to Support Comprehension

After paragraph 3: *Mr. Johns tells his two children, Keisha and Jamar, that they will be going on vacation.*

After paragraph 7: *Keisha is upset because she doesn't want to leave their puppy.*

After paragraph 10: *Jamar has an idea to start bringing the puppy to their grandma's house before the trip. That way, he can get used to her. And Jamar will teach his grandma how to send photos so they can keep in touch during vacation.*

After paragraph 12: *Keisha likes Jamar's idea. She starts to get excited about the vacation.*

CCSS
RL.2.1, L.2.1d, L.2.2a, L.2.3a

Objective

• Model making inferences/predictions

Set the Stage

Introduce the Text *Today I'm going to read aloud Part 1 of a fictional story that takes place thousands of years ago. It is about a young girl who never spoke to anyone except her mother, father, or grandmother because she was so shy. Over time, her grandmother teaches her a new craft in which she becomes skilled.*

Engage Thinking *What skill do you think the girl learns? Turn to a partner to share your prediction.*

Engage with the Text

Read aloud the text at a fluent, expressive pace. Use the suggested prompts to model your thinking, clarify events, and elicit student interaction.

1. *If I didn't know what the word "shy" meant, I could use context clues to figure it out. Based on the other sentences—"She never spoke to anyone" and "she would play alone"—I can determine that "shy" means "quiet" and "uncomfortable around others."* (Determine word meaning)

2. *In the phrase, "She sewed more rows," "sewed" and "rows" have the same /o/ sound. But "sewed" uses "ew" and "rows" uses "ow" for the same sound.* (Check spelling)

The Basket Weaver, Part 1

by Jacque Summer

1   Thousands of years ago, the Chumash People lived on the beautiful shores of California. And in the valley Aw'hay, there was a young girl named Yo'ee.

2   Yo'ee was very, very shy. She never spoke to anyone, except her mother, father, or grandmother. No one knew why Yo'ee was so shy, and neither did she. But every day she would play alone. **1**

3   One morning, Yo'ee's grandmother was sitting on the ground before the fire, weaving a basket. She saw Yo'ee playing. Yo'ee smiled as Grandmother waved her over to join her.

4   "Would you like to learn to make baskets?" her grandmother asked.

5   Yo'ee nodded. "I love baskets," she whispered.

6   Grandmother showed Yo'ee how to start the basket by wrapping juncus rushes with split reeds and stitching them into a beautiful, coiled base. After that she sewed more rows of reeds to the base. Her hands moved gracefully, like the wings of a bird. Yo'ee loved to watch her grandmother weave baskets. **2**

7   Yo'ee and Grandmother began to weave baskets together every day. Yo'ee helped her grandmother gather and prepare the reeds. They went down to the river and pulled bundles of slim, green stalks.

8   Some they would dry in the sun until they turned brown. The others they would soak in mud, turning them black as night before setting them out to dry. Then Yo'ee and Grandmother dipped the stiff reeds in water to soften them, and wove them into baskets. **3**

9   One day, as Yo'ee came back from the river with an armful of reeds, she heard the chief telling a story to the village children. The chief was not only a wise leader—he was a great storyteller. He spoke in a strong, clear voice that rose and fell like the river's song. The children listened as he told a story Yo'ee knew well. Coyote, Lizard, and Eagle, the first creatures of the earth, decided to make a new creature called man. But they could not decide on his hands.

10   "Proud Coyote wanted man to have hands like his," the chief said. He held up his own hands and curled them as if they were sharply clawed.

11   "Lizard and Eagle didn't argue, though Lizard knew Coyote was unwise. The next day, Coyote led the others to a white rock. If he stamped his paw on the rock, it would be final—humans would have hands just like the coyote.

12   "Lizard had to do something! He quickly crawled to the rock while Coyote wasn't looking and pressed his own tiny hand into the rock. Coyote was furious! But thanks to clever Lizard, we have useful hands with five fingers, just like him!" **4**

13   The children looked at their hands and laughed.

3. *Turn and talk to a partner. Recount the steps that Yo'ee and her grandmother took in order to prepare the reeds for the baskets.* (Summarize)

4. *After this great storyteller told his punchline, or the last line, I would expect the children to laugh, because they would probably know that it's not a true story but instead, a story that was meant to be humorous.* (Make inferences/predictions)

Extend Thinking Questions

Pose one or more questions to engage students more deeply with the text.

• *What made the chief such a great storyteller?*

• *What are some activities that you could do alone and sharpen a skill? Could you later teach someone else that skill?*

iELD Paraphrase to Support Comprehension

After paragraph 2: *A young girl named Yo'ee was very shy. She did not have any friends. She only spoke to her mother, father, and grandmother.*

After paragraph 7: *Yo'ee's grandmother taught her how to weave baskets.*

After paragraph 13: *All of the children in the village listened to the chief tell a story. His voice was strong and clear. He was a great storyteller.*

CCSS
RL.2.1, L.2.2d, L.2.4a, SL.2.2

Set the Stage

Introduce the Text *Today I'm going to read aloud Part 2 of "The Basket Weaver." In this story, Yo'ee has learned how to weave baskets from her grandmother. Part 1 ended with the village children laughing at the chief's story. Yo'ee wishes she could tell stories, too, and make people happy, but something is preventing her.*

Engage Thinking *Do you think Yo'ee can bring herself to be heard by the village? If so, how? Turn to a partner to share your prediction.*

Engage with the Text

Read aloud the text at a fluent, expressive pace. Use the suggested prompts to model your thinking, clarify events, and elicit student interaction.

1. *"She wished she could tell stories" could be written in other ways and still hold the same meaning. For instance, it could be rewritten as "Stories are what she wished she could tell." The original sentence could also be expanded to include an adjective, for instance: "She wished she could tell good stories."* (Rearrange sentences)

2. *Both "featherless" and "sadness" have root words I know, "feather" and "sad." But they both have suffixes as well, -less and -ness. If I knew that -less means "without" and -ness means "in the state or mood of," then I can determine that "featherless" means "without feathers," and "sadness" means "in the state of being sad" or "in a sad mood."* (Determine word meaning)

The Basket Weaver, Part 2

1 Yo'ee saw how the children loved to listen to the chief. She wished she could tell stories, too, to make others happy. But she was afraid. She thought her voice was too quiet to be heard. Still, she wanted to share the stories of her people. **1**

2 Then one day, as she was playing with a blue feather, she had an idea. She ran to tell her plan to Grandmother, who thought it was a wonderful idea. That minute they sat down and began working on a very special basket.

3 Soon it was time for the Acorn Harvest. Everyone in the village came together for the festival, eating, singing, and dancing. Yo'ee brought her new basket along.

4 After the feast, the chief asked if there were any who would like to tell a story. Yo'ee stood up, clutching her basket. Everyone was surprised. The chief nodded to her and sat down, ready to listen.

5 Yo'ee took a deep breath and held up her basket for all to see. On the first side of the basket, Yo'ee had woven a scrub jay. He was black and featherless, with his head cast down in sadness. **2** The people murmured, impressed by her handiwork. When everyone had seen the scrub jay, she turned the basket.

6 On the next side, the black jay was flying up to the basket's blue-feathered rim, as if asking the sky for some of its color. Yo'ee then turned the basket again. Now the sky dropped its blue feathers down to the jay. She turned the basket once more.

7 On the last side of the basket was the beautiful blue scrub jay, finally dressed in his sky-colored feathers. Yo'ee stood very still to show her story was over, then went back to sit by her grandmother. **3**

8 Everyone cheered at Yo'ee's tale. The chief stood and said, "Our village has another great storyteller. Next festival we look forward to another story from Yo'ee." **4**

9 Yo'ee's family hugged her proudly. Her grandmother's eyes twinkled.

10 "You've found a way to tell a story without speaking a word," she said to Yo'ee. "Your story was in the weaving of the basket."

11 And Yo'ee knew there would be plenty more stories to tell.

3. *Turn and talk to a partner. Ask and answer each other: How do you think the people in the village will respond to Yo'ee's form of storytelling?* (Make inferences/predictions/Ask questions)

4. *A compound word is made up of two individual words. The words "everyone" and "storyteller" are compound words: every+one and story+teller. They must mean "every person" and "teller of a story."* (Determine word meaning)

Extend Thinking Questions

Pose one or more questions to engage students more deeply with the text.

• *What made Yo'ee think she would not be a good storyteller? How did she overcome that fear and still manage to tell her story?*

• *Can you think of a weakness you might have? How could you use your skills to strengthen that weakness?*

iELD Paraphrase to Support Comprehension

After paragraph 1: *Yo'ee wanted to tell stories and make others happy. But she was afraid her voice was not loud enough.*

After paragraph 5: *Yo'ee planned to tell a story with one of her baskets. She wove the basket and took it to the village festival. The chief welcomed her to tell her story. She stood and showed her basket silently.*

After paragraph 11: *Yo'ee's story basket had been a success. Everyone was proud of her. Yo'ee was excited about weaving more story baskets.*

CCSS
RL.2.1, RF.2.3d, L.2.1f, L.2.4c, L.2.4d

Good Sports

1   It started out as a lazy day in the jungle. Cheetah, Lion, and Chameleon rested in the shade. Chimpanzee lounged in the crook of a tree. **1** Zebra stood nearby, grazing in the grass. Hippo had finished her morning swim and was sunning herself on the riverbank.

2   Only Giraffe was restless. With her head in the treetops, she couldn't help but notice the clear, blue sky peeking through the leaves. **2**

3   "It's such a beautiful day," said Giraffe, "and here we are just eating and sleeping. We should do something."

4   "What do you have in mind?" asked Cheetah.

5   Giraffe chewed thoughtfully on a leaf. "We could play a game."

6   "I like games," said Lion.

7   "Me, too," said Hippo.

8   "What kind of game?" asked Chimpanzee.

9   Giraffe thought about her favorite game. "We could play basketball," she suggested. She picked up a coconut and slam-dunked it between two very high branches. The coconut landed with a thud next to Cheetah.

10 Cheetah sat up. "Let's have a relay race." Cheetah stood up, stretched, and dashed toward a distant tree. He ran around the tree, then raced back to his friends.

11 Chameleon arose from her resting place, turning a bright green to match the surrounding leaves. "I know a fun game: hide-and-seek." Chameleon faded from green to brown then laid back down.

12 "I know a better game: soccer," exclaimed Zebra. He kicked a coconut. It went sailing over the branch where Chimpanzee was perched.

13 "I know something we could do: gymnastics." Chimpanzee did a backflip off the tree, landing next to Lion.

14 "Let's have a wrestling match," roared Lion. He took a playful swing at Hippo.

15 "I know what we could do. Let's go swimming," said Hippo. She put one foot in the water, splashing Giraffe.

16 "We should play basketball." Giraffe reached for another coconut.

17 "No, let's go swimming," said Hippo.

18 "Relay races," argued Cheetah.

19 "Hide-and-seek," insisted Chameleon.

20 Soon all the animals were shouting at once.

21 Elephant, who was wandering through the jungle in search of a playmate, heard the commotion. "Hello," he said, approaching the noisy group of animals. No one heard him above the shouting.

22 "Hello!" Elephant said a little louder. Still no one answered.

23 Elephant put down the small log he'd been carrying, threw his head back, and let out a mighty blast from his trunk. The noise shook the trees and sent several coconuts tumbling to the ground. Giraffe, Chameleon, Cheetah, Lion, Zebra, Hippo, and Chimpanzee stopped shouting and looked at Elephant.

24 Elephant picked up the log and swung at an imaginary ball. "Batter up, anyone?"

25 The animals stared at Elephant in silence.

26 Finally Chameleon spoke up. "I'm too small . . ." she began

27 "You could play shortstop," said Elephant. "You wouldn't have to throw very far."

28 "My arms are too long," said Chimpanzee.

29 "Perfect for throwing," said Elephant. "You could be the pitcher."

30 "Maybe I could be catcher," offered Hippo. "My thick skin would be good protection from the ball."

31 "I could be umpire," said Lion. He let out a roar. "No one would dare argue with my calls."

32 "I could play outfield," said Giraffe. "My long neck would give me a good view of the ball."

33 "Maybe I could be first at bat," said Cheetah. "I'm a great runner."

34 "I could play first base," said Zebra, and added, "that's my favorite position."

35 Chimpanzee scooped up an armful of coconuts. Cheetah gathered up four palm leaves for bases. Elephant led the animals in the direction of the clearing. Everyone got into position.

36 "Play ball!" called Elephant.

37 And that's just what they did. ④

Unit 4

3. *Turn and talk to a partner. Ask and answer each other: How do you think Elephant will get everyone's attention? (Make inferences/predictions/Ask questions)*

4. *All of these characters have their own personalities and points of view. How do their differences make the game more challenging? More interesting? (Ask questions)*

Extend Thinking Questions

Pose one or more questions to engage students more deeply with the text.

• *What game did Chameleon suggest they play? Why do you think she likes that game?*

• *If they all had to live in the same house together, how would you design it so that they could all be comfortable?*

iELD Paraphrase to Support Comprehension

After paragraph 9: *Giraffe suggested to her friends that they play a game. She wanted to play basketball.*

After paragraph 20: *The animals ended up shouting about wanting to play their choice of game.*

After paragraph 24: *Elephant walked up to the shouting animals. He made a loud trumpet noise to get their attention. He suggested they all play baseball.*

After paragraph 37: *All of the animals started thinking about what position would be best for them. Every animal was happy to play the game.*

CCSS
RL.2.1, RL.2.6, L.2.1b, L.2.4e

Objective
• Model summarizing/synthesizing

Set the Stage

Introduce the Text *Today I'm going to read aloud an informative article about how kids can invent—and why kids can even be good at it. It will give you tips on what you can do to get started with your own invention.*

Engage Thinking *Why do you think kids can be good at inventing? Turn to a partner to share your prediction.*

Engage with the Text

Read aloud the text at a fluent, expressive pace. Use the suggested prompts to model your thinking, clarify events, and elicit student interaction.

1. *You already know to capitalize someone's first and last name, as seen in "Cathy Kittinger." But did you also know to capitalize names of places, like "National Inventors Hall of Fame" and the city and state, "Akron, Ohio"?* (Capitalize names)

2. *The word "unique" is spelled like it should read uh-nih-kyoo. But it's an example of a word that you will recognize over time that you can't just sound out.* (Read irregularly spelled words)

Are You Meant to Invent?

by Karen Bradley Cain

1   You do not have to be grown up to be an inventor. Chester Greenwood was 15 when he invented earmuffs after ice skating made his ears cold. Benjamin Franklin fashioned the first swim paddles at the age of 10. And Thomas Edison started experimenting in his basement when he was only 10.

2   In fact, being young—or maybe just thinking like a youngster—may be an advantage. Children and inventors share a sense of curiosity about the world, according to Cathy Kittinger of the National Inventors Hall of Fame in Akron, Ohio. ❶

3   Young people also tend to be highly creative, according to Joshua Schuler, who runs a science program for students: "They're not as grounded by what is or is not possible. This is a terrific mind-set for an inventor." Invention is "about identifying and solving a problem in a unique or creative way," Schuler adds. ❷

4   Want to try your hand at inventing? Here are a few words of wisdom from the experts. Start with a bound notebook as your journal and record your ideas in pen. Then start brainstorming: What kind of invention are you looking to test and create? What would make life easier? Think about the things that annoy you. ❸   Schuler suggests considering the problems of less fortunate people. Write down all of your ideas and possible solutions.

5   Choose one invention, draw a model of it, and list what you will need to build it. Gather the tools—make sure you ask your parents first—and any necessary materials. If problems arise, keep in mind, as Schuler says, that "failure is an important part of the process."

6   When you have finished, decide what to call your invention. Some people get special permission, called a patent, to make, use, or sell their their invention. Young inventors should ask their parents and teachers about local and state invention programs. ❹

Benjamin Franklin

Thomas Edison

3. *It says to "think about the things that annoy you." Well, to "annoy" means to irritate, or make someone a little bit mad. Maybe some things that are annoying to you are having a little sister or brother who takes your stuff without permission, or stepping in chewing gum, or flies landing on your food.* (Make connections)

4. *Turn and talk to a partner. What is the main topic of this article? What does the last half of the article focus on?* (Summarize/synthesize)

Extend Thinking Questions

Pose one or more questions to engage students more deeply with the text.

• *What do experts say you should keep on hand if you want to start inventing?*

• *What would make life easier for you? for others?*

iELD Paraphrase to Support Comprehension

After paragraph 3: *Thinking like a young person is a great way to be creative. To a kid, anything is possible.*

After paragraph 4: *To invent, keep a notebook. Write or doodle all ideas in it. Include problems and possible answers.*

After paragraph 6: *There were problems with bartering and trading. You would have to carry everything with you, and you might not find anyone who had what you needed. Money is easier. You can carry it to stores and find exactly what you need.*

CCSS
RI.2.1, RI.2.2, L.2.2a, L.2.5a, RF.2.3f

Set the Stage

Introduce the Text *Today I'm going to read aloud the true story of the Wright brothers, named Orville and Wilbur, and how they became experts in the science of flying.*

Engage Thinking *What kind of toy do you think started the boys' interest in flying? Turn to a partner to share your prediction.*

Engage with the Text

Read aloud the text at a fluent, expressive pace. Use the suggested prompts to model your thinking, clarify events, and elicit student interaction.

1. *In the last sentence, "brought" and "began" are the past tense of irregular verbs. You have to do something other than add -ed to "bring" and "begin" in order to make them past tense.* (Use past tense of irregular verbs)

2. *I need to use context clues to figure out what "soaring" means. The sentence says that the brothers watched wing movements of soaring birds in order to design wings for their airplanes. I would think they would need to see the birds in flight to study how their wings moved, so "soaring" must mean "flying."* (Determine word meaning)

The Wright Brothers Take Off
by Mike Weinstein

1   Have you ever watched the hustle and bustle on an airport runway? Planes taking off. Baggage carts rumbling across the pavement. Planes easing up to the terminal. Mechanics fixing the planes. Did you know that all of this began when two young brothers, ages 7 and 11, started playing with a toy helicopter powered by a rubber band? Their father brought the toy home, and Wilbur and Orville Wright began their fascination with "flying machines." **1**

2   Twenty-five years later, in 1903, Wilbur and Orville Wright were grown men. On a cold and windy December day at the beach, the Wright brothers made the first successful flight in the world's first successful airplane. It was not a very long flight: It lasted only one minute. The flying machine looked more like a giant kite with propellers than an airplane. It jerked wildly in the strong breeze. Yet their feat stunned the world. Many people, at first, refused to believe it. But the world would never be the same again.

3   The Wrights' exciting day in Kitty Hawk, North Carolina, came after years of study, experimenting, and hard work. The brothers were good at fixing and building machines. As teenagers, they designed and built their own printing press. Then they became experts at repairing and building bicycles.

4   Neither brother finished high school, nor did they go to college. But they had inquiring minds. The brothers taught themselves the complex science of flying, which is called aviation. In part, they were inspired by watching vultures. When designing wings for their airplanes, they tried to copy the wing movements of the soaring birds. **2**

5   Wilbur and Orville designed and built a special machine—called a wind tunnel—to test different wing designs. Basically, this was a large fan blowing air through a rectangular box open at both ends. After several months of testing, the Wright brothers became experts on airplane design.

6   Orville and Wilbur counted on one another for their success. They were so close, in the ways that they felt and thought, that they were almost like twins. Sometimes, they discussed and shared thoughts over the course of many days and months. Their exchange of ideas often produced brilliant answers to difficult problems.

7   Their flying experiments required physical strength and courage. During their tests at Kitty Hawk, the brothers slept and lived on the beach. The frequent winds and soft sand for landings made Kitty Hawk good for flying. But it could be hard living. Kitty Hawk's insects and harsh winds made life a challenge.

8   After their successful flights in 1903, the Wrights returned to their home in Dayton. They spent a few years there quietly testing, practicing, and improving their airplanes. Within a few years, Wilbur was traveling to Europe to show off the brothers' newest airplane. **3** Meanwhile, Orville was demonstrating an airplane to the U.S. government.

9   Wilbur died in 1912 at age 45, nine years after the first flight at Kitty Hawk. Orville lived another 36 years, until 1948. He lived long enough to see airplanes help win World War II, fly across oceans, and carry millions of travelers around the country each year. **4**

---

3. *There is an apostrophe after "brothers" because that word is a possessive noun. That means that the brothers own what comes after that word: newest airplane. The brothers own the airplane.* (Use apostrophes)

4. *Turn and talk to a partner. Take turns saying one sentence each, starting with the brothers as children, and summarize what happened to them throughout their lives, sentence by sentence.* (Summarize/synthesize)

Extend Thinking Questions

Pose one or more questions to engage students more deeply with the text.

• *What important event occurred in December 1903 in Kitty Hawk, North Carolina? How long did it last?*

• *What kind of bird does the article say the brothers studied to help with understanding flight?*

iELD Paraphrase to Support Comprehension

After paragraph 1: *As young boys, a toy helicopter started the Wright brothers' interest in flying.*

After paragraph 2: *The Wright brothers flew the world's first plane in 1903 for one minute.*

After paragraph 5: *The Wright brothers studied hard and experimented to figure out how machines work. They also built a wind tunnel to test wing designs.*

After paragraph 6: *Orville and Wilbur worked together closely.*

After paragraph 9: *Orville Wright lived long enough to see how airplanes changed the world.*

CCSS
RI.2.1, RI.2.2, RI.2.4, L.2.1d, L.2.2c, L.2.4a, SL.2.1a

Unit 5

Willy Wriggler's Wheels

by Kathleen M. Muldoon

1   Willy Wriggler wanted wheels. He was tired of slithering around City Park on his belly. Every day Willy watched people whiz by on wheels—boys and girls on scooters and skateboards, babies in strollers, messengers on bicycles, gardeners riding lawn mowers, children on roller skates . . .

2   It seemed as if everyone except Willy had wheels.

3   "I'll visit Roy D. Rat," Willy said. "He'll help me get wheels."

4   Roy D. Rat lived in a hollow log across from Willy Wriggler's rock. He didn't have wheels, but he could run fast on his four legs. He didn't have to wriggle like Willy.

5   Willy slithered along while Roy skipped beside him. They passed trucks and cars. They passed wheelchairs and carriages and motorcycles. They passed skaters and cyclists.

6   The park was filled with wheels—wheels that were attached to someone or something. There were no loose wheels for Willy.

7   Roy and Willy reached the far corner of the park where workers had recently built new skateboard ramps. Whiz! Whoosh! WHAM!

8   Skateboarders raced up and down the concrete slopes. Each wore a brightly colored helmet. Pink helmets and red helmets. Blue helmets and gold helmets. Green helmets and purple helmets.

9   Their heads bobbed like brightly colored balloons as they leaped and dipped on their skateboards.

10 From beneath a nearby bench, Willy and Roy watched the skateboarders until the park closed.

11 Willy sighed.

12 "Just once I'd like to ride a skateboard," he said. "They're the perfect size and shape for me, long and flat."

13 As Willy and Roy D. Rat headed home, the moon peeked out suddenly from behind a cloud and shined on four silver wheels lying by the side of the path. Willy slithered over. Upside down in the grass lay a discarded skateboard.

14 "Wheels!" he exclaimed.

15 Roy D. Rat scurried over to examine the board.

16 "It's cracked," he said. "But it's perfect for you, Willy. Come on. Let's try it out."

17 Roy pushed the skateboard to the top of the concrete ramp. Willy wriggled behind him. **3**

18 "Get on!" Roy ordered.

19 "Wait," Willy said. He searched in the grass until he found what he needed, an acorn cap just his size. It made a perfect helmet. Now he was ready.

20 Carefully, he slithered aboard the skateboard. The crack cradled his body and held it securely in a straight line down the center of the board.

21 "Launch me to the moon!" he cried to Roy.

22 With a gentle push, Roy started Willy rushing down the ramp on his wheels.

23 "COWABUNGA!" Willy shouted to the heavens.

24 WHOOSH! He held his breath as he zoomed to the bottom of the ramp.

25 WHIZZZZZ! Willy shrieked in delight as his board climbed to the top of the opposite ramp, which sat just beneath the moon.

26 "ALLEY OOOOOOOOOOP!" he shouted as the board went backward down one ramp and up another. Immediately the board headed back down. Up and down, backward and forward. Willy wriggled happily as he flew on his wheels.

27 At last he came to a stop in the gully between the ramps. Roy D. Rat scampered down to greet him.

28 "How was it?" he asked.

29 "Awesome," Willy said. "I've been to the moon and back, all in one night."

30 Roy pushed Willy and his wheels back up the ramp. Then together Roy and Willy hid Willy's wheels under a nearby shrub to await his next ride.

31 If you're ever in City Park on a moonlit night, you may get a glimpse of Willy Wriggler whooshing and whamming, leaping and dipping on his very own wheels. Just look for his acorn helmet and his able assistant, Roy D. Rat. **4**

3. *The "R" in "Roy" and the "wr" in "wriggled" have the same /r/ sound. So if I see other "wr" words, they will probably have the same /r/ sound.* (Generalize learned spelling patterns)

4. *Turn and talk to a partner. Retell the story by summarizing the important parts of how Willy made it to the moon and back, starting with his visit to Roy D. Rat.* (Summarize/synthesize)

Extend Thinking Questions

Pose one or more questions to engage students more deeply with the text.

• *What kind of animal do you picture Willy to be, and why?*

• *Why was a skateboard the perfect wheeled object for Willy, and what made the crack in it even better?*

iELD Paraphrase to Support Comprehension

After paragraph 6: *Willy wanted to ride on wheels instead of slithering on his belly. He went to a park and saw plenty of wheels, but they were all being used.*

After paragraph 13: *Willy was slithering home when he noticed a skateboard. Nobody was using it.*

After paragraph 20: *Willy made a helmet out of an acorn cap. The crack in the skateboard held his body in place.*

After paragraph 29: *Willy rode the skateboard back and forth, up and down two ramps. He felt like he was going to the moon every time he went up. He loved the ride.*

CCSS
RL.2.1, RF.2.3a, L.2.1e, L.2.2d, SL.2.2

Set the Stage

Introduce the Text *Today I'm going to read aloud two letters written to a newspaper. The first letter complains about people's use of phones for texting, while the next letter supports texting.*

Engage Thinking *Can you think of one reason why someone might be against using cell phones for texting?*

Engage with the Text

Read aloud the text at a fluent, expressive pace. Use the suggested prompts to model your thinking, clarify events, and elicit student interaction.

1. *In the letter, "careful" is an adjective that describes how we should act when using this new technology.* (Use phrases with adjectives)

2. *"Myself" is a reflexive pronoun that is used to refer to what comes before it. Reflexive pronouns end with "self" or "selves."* (Use reflexive pronouns)

Texting: Yes or No?

1   Dear *Star Journal* Editor:

I'm writing to complain about all of the people who I see out on the street texting on their cell phones. I think this is dangerous and that something needs to be done to stop this. I saw a woman the other day who almost walked into a telephone pole! She was so busy typing into her phone that she didn't watch where she was going!

I know that cell phones are a useful technology, but do we need to use them every minute of every day? We have to be careful **1** about how we use this new technology. Only ten years ago you would have never seen something like this on the streets. People could get from one place to another without sending messages and looking at their phones.

I think we should return to the days when people would think about what they are doing. Stop texting now! Let's do just one thing at a time!

We don't want to increase accidents and have people get hurt! I am hoping the town can create a new law that keeps the texts quiet. I think that would keep us all a little safer.

Sincerely,

Concerned Citizen

2 Dear *Star Journal* Editor:

I just read a letter from a reader named "Concerned Citizen," who hoped that laws could be made to stop people from sending texts in the streets. I think that would be a bad idea. It's true that people can be careless when they text in public. But cell phones and texting are important.

Cell phones and texts can keep people safe. People can reach each other wherever they are. They can help in an emergency. A written text keeps someone from being bothered. They can read the text later if they are busy.

Texts are a great idea that solve many problems! I would love to thank the person who invented texting, instead of telling him or her that we don't want to allow it in our town.

As a "concerned citizen" myself, **2** I think keeping people from using new technologies can be dangerous. If we want to grow and learn, we should use new technologies. We just need to make sure people learn how to use it safely. Let's make people aware of the dangers of texting and walking instead of telling them they cannot use their phones. Let's learn to use technology correctly!

Sincerely, **3**

Technology Fan **4**

3. *There is a comma used in the closing of a letter, before the name is signed.* (Use commas)

4. *Turn and talk to a partner. One of you should give the reasons that the first letter stated for not using phones to text. The other partner should give the reasons stated in the second letter for supporting texting.* (Summarize/synthesize)

Extend Thinking Questions

Pose one or more questions to engage students more deeply with the text.

• *Do you think the people who developed texting agree more with the points made by Concerned Citizen or Technology Fan?*

• *If you were going to text someone, when and where might be a good place to do it? When could be a bad time, and why?*

Unit 5

iELD Paraphrase to Support Comprehension

After letter 1: *A writer is concerned about cell phone texting. He or she is worried that people could hurt themselves and others while texting. The writer wants a new law against texting.*

After letter 2: *In response to the first letter, another writer supports texting. He or she thinks there is value in allowing texting. The writer supports teaching people of the dangers of texting instead.*

CCSS
RI.2.1, RI.2.2, RI.2.4, L.2.1c, L.2.2b, L.2.6, SL.2.1a

The Traffic Signal:
A Bright Idea from a Bright Inventor

1   Garrett Morgan was born in Kentucky in 1877. He was the first African American inventor in the United States. Even though he did not get more than an elementary school education, Garrett was always thinking and working very hard. When he grew up **1** and moved to Ohio, he hired a tutor to help him learn as much as he could.

2   Garrett was always good at fixing things. He worked as a sewing machine repairman. After a while, he opened his own repair shop for sewing machines. All the time Garrett was working, he thought about new inventions and ideas.

3   One of Garrett's most interesting inventions was the Morgan Traffic Signal. In the early 1900s, cars were just beginning to become popular. Cars got into accidents a lot. New cars, older horse-drawn carriages, and people all shared the same roads. There were many accidents. No one had yet invented a way to let cars know when they should stop and let another car go ahead. There were no sidewalks for people to walk on. **2**

4   Other people had tried to invent traffic signals. However, Garrett's idea worked well. And, it was not expensive to make them for towns across the country. In fact, Garrett's traffic signal was used throughout all of the United States for many years. **3**

5   Garrett's traffic signal was a T-shaped pole with three signals. "Stop" meant that cars would have to stop where the streets crossed each other. "Go" meant that it was time for cars to go while others waited. The third position of the signal was a "Stop" in all directions. It meant that all traffic in the street had to stop. This signal meant that people could safely use the street without having to worry about cars moving in any direction.

6   Garrett invented other things, too. Like the traffic signal, many of his inventions were meant to keep people safe. Today there are many more cars and people on the roads than ever. Garrett Morgan's ideas for traffic safety were the beginning of a long line of safety inventions for the car. Hopefully inventions like these will continue for many years to come. **4**

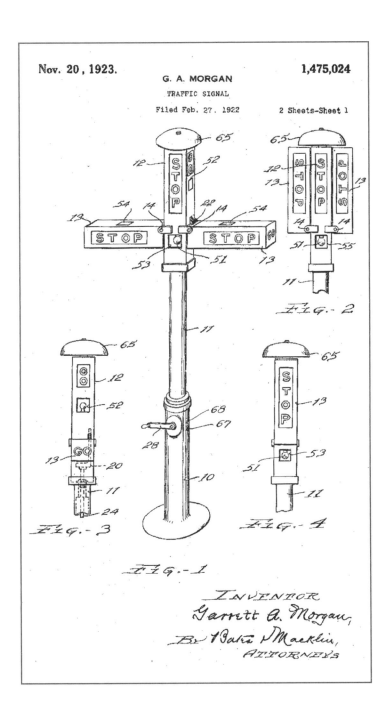

Nov. 20, 1923.

G. A. MORGAN

TRAFFIC SIGNAL

Filed Feb. 27, 1922

1,475,024

2 Sheets-Sheet 1

FIG.-2

FIG.-3

FIG.-4

FIG.-1

INVENTOR
Garrett A. Morgan,
By Baker Macklin,
ATTORNEYS

3. *"United States" is capitalized because it is the name of a country, which is a geographic name.* (Capitalize geographic names)

4. *Turn and talk to a partner. Identify the main topic of the article. Then summarize the important parts of the article.* (Summarize/synthesize)

Extend Thinking Questions

Pose one or more questions to engage students more deeply with the text.

• *Why was it important in the past for car traffic to stop in all directions?*

• *Garrett Morgan created many inventions to keep people safe. What is a safety concern that you might have?*

iELD Paraphrase to Support Comprehension

After paragraph 2: *Garrett Morgan was born in 1877. He grew to become a famous African American inventor in the United States. Garrett learned as much as he could. He worked with sewing machines. But he had a lot of ideas for inventions.*

After paragraph 4: *Garrett wanted to keep people from getting in accidents in the streets. He created a traffic signal that helped with the problem. It was used around the country for years.*

Unit 5

CCSS
RI.2.1, RI.2.4, RI.2.6, L.2.1d, L.2.2a, L.2.4d

Objective

• Model making connections

Set the Stage

Introduce the Text *Today I'm going to read aloud a folktale that is a popular story told in West Africa. It is about a man who had three sons and owned a valuable cow.*

Engage Thinking *How do you think the man made money? Turn to a partner to share your prediction.*

Engage with the Text

Read aloud the text at a fluent, expressive pace. Use the suggested prompts to model your thinking, clarify events, and elicit student interaction.

1. *If I wanted to use context clues to figure out what "furious" means, I could read the following sentences. They describe him yelling and throwing his son out of his house. I can tell that "furious" means he is very mad.* (Determine word meaning)

2. *The man calls the cow "precious." That is another way of saying "loved" or "dear" or even something that could never be made again if broken. For example, a baby is often called precious. Or a handmade quilt from a loved one. Or even jewels are sometimes called precious.* (Make connections)

3. *The folktale repeats lines in order to give the story rhythm and meaning. An important line repeats: it is when the man asks the cow if she's had enough to eat and drink. This shows how badly he wants to please the cow. When the man asks the same question after caring for the cow himself, he realizes the cow has lied every time.* (Determine text importance)

A Man and His Precious Cow

A Folktale from West Africa

1   Many years ago, a man lived with three sons and one cow. Every year, the cow gave birth to a health baby calf. Every year, the man sold the calf at the market. The man felt very lucky to have such a great cow.

2   One day, the man asked his oldest son to care for the cow.

3   "Make sure it eats only the best grass and the best water," he commanded.

4   So the eldest son led the cow to grassy fields. Then he took it to a cool watering hole.

5   Later, the man asked his cow, "Dearest cow, did you have enough to eat and to drink?"

6   "Not at all!" the cow complained. "Your rotten son took me to the desert. There was no grass, and the ground was dry as a stone!"

7   The man was furious. ❶ He yelled, "How could you treat our precious cow so horribly!" The man threw his oldest son out of the house. The son did not know what to do, so he began to walk. Eventually, he came to a farmhouse. The kind farmer welcomed him into his home and taught him how to farm.

8   The next day, the man called for his second son. He said, "Make sure our precious cow gets the best grass and the best water!" ❷

9   So the eldest son led the cow to grassy fields. Then he took it to a cool pond.

10   Later, the man asked his cow, "Dearest cow, did you have enough to eat and to drink?"

11   "Not at all!" the cow complained. "Your rotten son took me to the desert. Again, there was no grass and no water!"

12   The man yelled at his second son, "You, too, are no longer allowed to live here!" The second son went off. Eventually, he met a blacksmith who welcomed him into his home and taught him how to make metal shovels.

13 The next day, the man called for his youngest son. "Son, you have always been my favorite. Please take good care of our cow. If you do not, I will have to send you away like your brothers. And that would break my heart."

14 So the youngest son took the cow to the best grass and to the freshest stream.

15 Later, the man asked his cow, "Dearest cow, did you have enough to eat and to drink?"

16 "Not at all!" the cow complained. "Your favorite son is more rotten than the others. He rode on my back. I had nothing to eat or to drink."

17 The man's heart sank. But he believed every word. The youngest son set off. Eventually, he came to a house where he met a kind teacher, who taught him how to read and write.

18 All alone, the man took the cow to lush fields and to the coldest ponds. Finally, he asked the cow, "Dearest cow, did you have enough to eat and drink?"

19 "Not at all!" the cow complained. "I've not had a bite to eat or a sip to drink all day. You treat me worse than your rotten sons!"

20 The man could not believe his ears. The cow had been lying to him all along. ❸

21 He yelled, "Go! Find your own grass and water!" Then the man began walking. He looked everywhere for his sons but did not find them.

22 Weeks passed, and it was time to go to the market. But he was so tired and so sad that he leaned against the market gate crying, "Oh, what have I done? I sent my boys away. I no longer have a cow. I no longer have a calf. I have no money and no food." He wailed and cried out. People at the market noticed the man. A crowd gathered around him.

23 Suddenly, voices cried out from the crowd, "Papa! Papa! Papa!" The eldest son had come to market to sell foods from the farm. The second son had come to sell metal shovels. The third son had come to find books. All three boys were so happy. They rushed to him.

24 The man wept with joy when he saw his three sons.

25 "Forgive me, please!" he asked. "My dear sons, you are more precious to me than a cow." ❹

4. *Turn and talk to a partner. Retell the folktale and its moral. (Summarize)*

Extend Thinking Questions

Pose one or more questions to engage students more deeply with the text.

• *Why did the man want to please the cow?*

• *Why does the man ask for forgiveness?*

iELD Paraphrase to Support Comprehension

After paragraph 7: *A man told his oldest son to care for his only cow. The son did. The man asked his cow if she was fed well. The cow lied and said no. The man believed the cow and kicked his son out of his home.*

After paragraph 12: *The man asked his second son to care for his cow. The boy did. Again, the cow lied. The man forced this son to move.*

After paragraph 17: *The man asked his last son to care for the cow. The boy did. The cow lied again. The man was very sad and believed the cow. He kicked his son out.*

After paragraph 21: *The man fed the cow too. He asked the cow if she had enough. The cow lied once more. The man realized that the cow had lied all along. The man was mad. He ordered the cow to go away and searched for his sons.*

After paragraph 25: *He missed his sons. All of his sons were at the market that day. They were so happy to see him. The man asked to be forgiven.*

CCSS
RL.2.1, RL.2.2, RL.2.4, L.2.4a, L.2.5a

Unit 6

Happy New Year!

by Pat Sandifer Borum

New day.

New year.

Happy times

Are here.

5 "Bye" to the old.

"Hi" to the new.

May wishes and dreams

Come true for you.

Chinese New Year

by Jacqueline Schiff

Sweep the bad luck out the door.

Scrub, scrub, scrub the kitchen floor.

Dust and tidy every room,

Chinese New Year's coming soon.

5   Hang the banners on the wall,

With good wishes meant for all.

Dance like lions. Drum with joy.

In Chinese, sing, "Gung hay fat choy!"

---

4. *Turn and talk to a partner. Ask each other: In what ways are Americans and Chinese similar in getting ready for the New Year? Different?* (Make connections/Ask questions)

Extend Thinking Questions

Pose one or more questions to engage students more deeply with the text.

• *What do Chinese people do before celebrating the New Year by dancing and singing?*

• *How does your family celebrate the New Year? How is it similar to either of these cultures?*

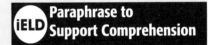

iELD Paraphrase to Support Comprehension

After poem 1: *This poem describes how easily the New Year comes in the United States. No preparation is necessary to ring in the upcoming year. Just say "bye" to the past year. The author wishes happiness and dreams come true for your New Year.*

After poem 2: *This poem describes all of the work that is done to clean the home before ringing in the New Year in China. It represents getting rid of any past bad luck. After all of the cleaning has been done, the Chinese get ready to dance and sing and celebrate the New Year.*

Unit 6

CCSS
RL.2.1, RL.2.4, L.2.1f, L.2.2c

Brother Tiger and the Well
A Folktale from Costa Rica, Part 1
Retold by William Kelly

1 ANANSI DANGLED FROM his web high in the cacao tree, trying to cool off in the steamy rain forest air. Through the busy chatter of parrots and toucans, he heard a faint cry.

2 "Help!" came the faraway voice of Brother Tiger. "Someone help me, please!"

3 Anansi spun out a line of thread and dropped between the big cacao leaves. Then he scurried along an overgrown trail, following Brother Tiger's troubled cries until he reached the banana farm. **1**

4 "Oh, please help me!" Brother Tiger's voice sounded quite near. Anansi looked up and down the shadowy green rows of banana trees. But the tiger was nowhere to be seen.

5 "Where are you, Brother Tiger?" Anansi shouted.

6 "Down here!" Brother Tiger's voice rose out of an old stone well. "Please save me, Anansi!"

7 Anansi scrambled over the side of the well and peered down into the dark opening. Two sad yellow eyes gazed back up at him.

8 "I fell in trying to get a drink," wailed Brother Tiger. "I've been down here for such a long time! I'm cold and wet, and I'm hungry, too. If you get me out I'll do anything you ask—anything at all. I promise!"

9 "You're a long way down," Anansi said, "and my thread isn't strong enough to pull you up."

10 "But you're a clever little spider," Brother Tiger pleaded. "If anyone can figure out a way to save me, you can."

11 Anansi sat at the edge of the well, thinking. Brother Tiger's sobs echoed in the darkness below.

12 "I've got it!" Anansi said finally. "Be patient, Brother Tiger—I'll be right back!"

13 Anansi scurried home to his cacao tree and called out for the one creature who could help in this situation. "Brother Monkey! Brother Monkey—I need you!" **2**

14 In a flash, Brother Monkey appeared, jumping and twirling in excitement. "What do you want, Anansi?"

15 "Will you help me save Brother Tiger?" asked Anansi. "He fell in the well at the banana farm and can't get out!"

16 "A rescue! Oh, how exciting!" Brother Monkey hopped up and down, his long tail curling and uncurling. "Climb on my back, and I'll take you there!"

17 Anansi let himself down on a thread and grabbed onto Brother Monkey's neck. Off they went, hurtling through the lush, green rain forest. Soon they arrived at the well, where they could hear Brother Tiger whimpering.

18 "Listen up, Brother Tiger!" shouted Anansi. "Brother Monkey and I are here to help you. Brother Monkey will hang down into the well and lower his tail to you. You must take hold of his tail gently with your mouth and climb while he pulls you up."

19 "Whatever you say, Anansi," said Brother Tiger in a hopeful voice. **3**

20 Brother Monkey lowered his tail. The tiger carefully took it in his mouth, then pressed his four paws against the sides of the well and slowly began clawing his way up.

21 "Pull, Brother Monkey," Anansi shouted. "Pull as hard as you can!"

22 "He's so heavy," said Brother Monkey with a grimace. "But he's coming up now!"

23 Brother Monkey struggled over the edge of the well. Sure enough, the tiger's head soon appeared. His lips were clamped firmly around Brother Monkey's tail.

24 "Just a wee bit further," Anansi encouraged the cold, wet tiger. "Now hook your paws on top of the well and pull yourself over!"

25 Still holding on to the monkey's tail, Brother Tiger hauled himself up and tumbled onto the ground.

26 "Hurrah!" cheered Anansi. **4**

3. *The word "hopeful" has the root word "hope." The suffix -ful is added to the end of the root word. "Hopeful" describes the way the tiger's voice sounded at the thought of getting rescued: full of hope.* (Determine word meaning)

4. *Turn and talk to a partner. Retell Part 1 of the folktale, giving facts and details that help "paint the picture." Be sure to use complete sentences and speak clearly.* (Summarize)

Extend Thinking Questions

Pose one or more questions to engage students more deeply with the text.

• *Based on his response, why did Brother Monkey decide to help save Brother Tiger?*

• *The tiger promised to do anything the spider asked of him, if only Anansi got him out. Have you ever promised something in return for getting what you want?*

iELD Paraphrase to Support Comprehension

After paragraph 8: *A tiger fell in a hole called a well. He called out for help. A spider came. The tiger told the spider he would do anything for him if he could get him out.*

After paragraph 19: *The spider called on a monkey to help. The spider told the tiger what to do in order to get out. The tiger would have to grab the monkey's tail with his mouth and be pulled out. The tiger agreed to try it.*

After paragraph 26: *The spider cheered them on as the monkey pulled the tiger out. It worked! The spider was happy for the tiger.*

CCSS
RL.2.1, L.2.2d, L.2.4c, SL.2.4

Set the Stage

Introduce the Text *Today I'm going to read aloud Part 2 of the Costa Rican folktale about the tiger who had fallen down a well. Where we left off, the monkey had just pulled out the cold, wet, hungry tiger.*

Engage Thinking *What do you think will happen now that the tiger is out? Turn to a partner to share your prediction.*

Engage with the Text

Read aloud the text at a fluent, expressive pace. Use the suggested prompts to model your thinking, clarify events, and elicit student interaction.

1. *The verb "give" is irregular. That means you can't just add -ed to the end of the root verb to form the past tense. Instead, "give" becomes "gave" for the past tense form of the verb.* (Use past tense of irregular verbs)

2. *Anansi is speaking to Brother Tiger in a calm voice. I know that when I am calm, I can think and focus better. Maybe Anansi is trying to keep calm so that it will calm the hungry tiger down, too. And it will give Anansi a chance to think up a plan to save the monkey.* (Make connections)

3. *The monkey "darted" straight to the tree, and he "scrambled" to the top. The two verbs, "darted" and "scrambled," are closely related. They both mean that the monkey was going as fast as he could. However there is a slight difference in meaning. When he "darted," he moved suddenly and quickly with nothing slowing him down. And when he "scrambled," there was a bit of struggle involved.* (Distinguish shades of meaning)

Brother Tiger and the Well
A Folktale from Costa Rica, Part 2

1   "Hurrah!" cheered Brother Monkey.

2   But Brother Tiger did not cheer. He placed his huge right paw on top of Brother Monkey, pinning him to the ground. Only then did he open his mouth and let go of Brother Monkey's tail.

3   "Brother Tiger, what are you doing?" asked Anansi.

4   The tiger didn't respond. He gave Brother Monkey a hungry look.

5   "He's going to eat me!" screamed Brother Monkey.

6   "Not yet," said Anansi in a calm voice. "First he has to keep a promise he made to me. He said he'd do anything I asked if I got him out of the well—isn't that right, Brother Tiger?"

7   "Yes, yes," said Brother Tiger impatiently. "And I will keep my promise—so long as you don't ask me to let this monkey go!"

8   "No," agreed Anansi, "I will not ask that."

9   "Aieeee!" cried Brother Monkey. "I saved you, Brother Tiger! You can't eat me! What are you saying, Anansi?"

10 "This is what I am saying," answered Anansi calmly. "Brother Tiger, are you ready to keep your promise?" **2**

11 "If you insist," said Brother Tiger with a sigh. "Let's get this promise out of the way so I can have my supper! What is it that you want me to do?"

12 "Raise your right paw and repeat after me," said Anansi. "I swear on my stripes that I will never go near this well again."

13 "Is that all!" said Brother Tiger. He held up his right paw and began, "I swear on my stripes—"

14 But the moment Brother Monkey felt the tiger's paw lift, he darted straight to the nearest banana tree. He scrambled all the way to the top and sat on a branch, shrieking and hollering and shaking his fist at Brother Tiger. **3**

15 "Thank you, Brother Tiger," said Anansi with a grin. "Now you can have your supper—but I do believe you'll be dining alone this evening!"

16 Brother Tiger scowled and growled and twitched his tail as he slunk away into the rain forest.

17 From that time on, Brother Monkey refused to come down out of the treetops when Brother Tiger was around. Even to this day, monkeys do not trust tigers.

18 And this is why all monkeys choose to live high in the tops of the rain forest trees. ❹

4. *Turn and talk to a partner. Ask each other any questions you may have about the story. Try to answer each other's questions. After you have done that, then tell each other what Anansi means by saying, "You'll be dining alone."* (Ask questions)

Extend Thinking Questions

Pose one or more questions to engage students more deeply with the text.

• *How did Anansi tell the tiger to let the monkey go without actually saying "Let the monkey go"?*

• *The fact that the tiger promised the spider anything he wanted came in handy for the monkey. What does this folktale show about Anansi's character?*

iELD Paraphrase to Support Comprehension

After paragraph 5: *The hungry tiger pinned the monkey to the ground. He was about to eat him.*

After paragraph 13: *The spider told the tiger he needed to keep his promise before eating. The tiger said he would. He would do anything except let the monkey go. The spider tricked the tiger into raising his paw off the monkey.*

After paragraph 18: *The monkey climbed up a tree. The tiger walked off. The monkey never trusted the tiger again.*

Unit 6

CCSS
RL.2.1, RL.2.2, L.2.1d, L.2.5b, SL.2.3

Set the Stage

Introduce the Text *Today I'm going to read aloud Sijo poems from Korea. Sijo is an ancient form of poetry.*

Engage Thinking *What is one thing found in nature that you think could be appreciated? Turn to a partner to share your thoughts.*

Engage with the Text

Read aloud the text at a fluent, expressive pace. Use the suggested prompts to model your thinking, clarify events, and elicit student interaction.

1. *"Snowfall" is a compound word made of two individual words, "snow" and "fall." The word means "snow that has fallen." I can tell because the poem says it makes a blanket on the mountain village.* (Determine word meaning)

2. *I would like to check the spelling of "crescent." I look through my dictionary and see that it's listed after "crescendo." I read in the definition that "c-r-e-s-c-e-n-t" is a phase of the moon, so I know that it's spelled correctly.* (Check spellings)

3. *"Disappeared" uses the prefix -dis. That prefix means "do the opposite of." I already know that "appeared" is the past tense of "appear," which means "arrive." So altogether, "disappeared" must mean "did the opposite of arrive," or "went away."* (Determine word meaning)

Sijo Poems

Sijo poems are an ancient form of writing from Korea. These poems often do not have titles. Each one is exactly three lines long with about fourteen to sixteen syllables per line.

1   Snowfall blankets the mountain village and buries my rocky lane. **1**

     No need to open the brushwood gate, none will come to see me.

     Still a crescent moon **2** smiles brightly down, the truest friend I have.

                          —*Sin Hum*

2   The spring breeze melted snow on the hills then quickly disappeared. **3**

     I wish I could borrow it briefly to blow over my hair

     And melt away the aging frost forming now about my ears.

                          – *U Tak*

3   You ask how many friends I have? Water and stone, bamboo and pine.

     The moon rising over the eastern hill is a joyful comrade.

     Besides these five companions, what other pleasure should I ask? **4**

                          –*Yun Seondo*

4. *Turn and talk to a partner. Explain how the five natural elements that the author listed could be friends.* (Make connections)

Extend Thinking Questions

Pose one or more questions to engage students more deeply with the text.

• *How do you think the author of the second Sijo poem, U Tak, feels about his age?*

• *If Yun Seondo had no human friends, how do you think he would feel?*

iELD Paraphrase to Support Comprehension

After poem 1: *Snow covers the lane to the author's house. Nobody is coming to visit. The moonlight shines regularly, so the author considers the moon something to appreciate.*

After poem 2: *Time is passing. The author wishes he could use the breeze to blow some hair over his balding head and melt away the gray hairs on his ears. He wishes to look younger again.*

After poem 3: *The author is happy with being alone, as long as he has the moon, water, stones, bamboo, and pine.*

Unit 6

CCSS
RL.2.1, RL.2.4, L.2.2e, L.2.4b, L.2.4d

Set the Stage

Introduce the Text *Today I'm going to read aloud a poem by a famous poet, Jack Prelutsky. He tells us not to bother looking for something that used to live long ago.*

Engage Thinking *What do you think the author tells us not to look for? Turn to a partner to share your prediction.*

Engage with the Text

Read aloud the text at a fluent, expressive pace. Use the suggested prompts to model your thinking, clarify events, and elicit student interaction.

1. *I am wondering what "extinct" means. I will use a dictionary to help me figure it out. Reading through all of the definitions, I can tell that it means "no longer living." So "long-extinct" must mean that it stopped living long ago.* (Determine word meaning)

2. *The poem so far has a rhythm to it. There is the same number of syllables in each line (eight). And the end of each line rhymes, making it flow smoothly.* (Supply rhythm with beats and rhymes)

Long Gone

by Jack Prelutsky

Don't waste your time in looking for

The long-extinct tyrannosaur,

Because this ancient dinosaur

Just can't be found here anymore.

5   This also goes for stegosaurus,

Allosaurus, brontosaurus

And any other saur or saurus.

They all lived here long before us.

3. *I need to stop and think about what a "saur or saurus" is because I've never heard of that before. If I read the poem again, I can see that all of the dinosaurs that have been listed so far all end in "saur or saurus," so that must refer to all the other dinosaurs that the author hasn't listed in the poem.* (Use fix-up monitoring strategies)

4. *Turn and talk to a partner. Tell how the poem begins and ends. What is the author trying to tell you?* (Determine structure)

Extend Thinking Questions

Pose one or more questions to engage students more deeply with the text.

• *What lived long ago?*

• *If we shouldn't bother looking for dinosaurs, should we bother with knowing about them?*

iELD **Paraphrase to Support Comprehension**

After stanza 1: *Tyrannosaurus is a kind of dinosaur. They lived long ago. They are no longer here. Don't bother looking for them.*

After stanza 2: *No other dinosaur is alive today. Don't look for the others, either.*

Unit 7

CCSS
RL.2.1, RL.2.4, RL.2.5, L.2.4e

Objective

• Model fix-up monitoring strategies

Set the Stage

Introduce the Text *Today I'm going to read aloud an article that was written by a dinosaur detective, called a paleontologist. She is someone who takes the bones that people find and puts them together to create a whole dinosaur model.*

Engage Thinking *What kinds of tools do you think she uses to clean the bones and chip away the dirt and rock surrounding them? Turn to a partner to share your prediction.*

Engage with the Text

Read aloud the text at a fluent, expressive pace. Use the suggested prompts to model your thinking, clarify events, and elicit student interaction.

1. *The word "fossilized" has the root word "fossil," which is from something that lived long ago. I know that the suffix -ize means "to become." The "d" on the very end makes the word past tense. So the sentence is saying that the bones have become fossils.* (Determine word meaning)

2. *The word "don't" is a contraction, which is a shortened word due to missing letters. In this case, the "o" is missing from "not" and the apostrophe is taking its place. So, "don't" means "do not."* (Use apostrophes)

Dana Daring: Dino Detective

This read-aloud is from the point-of-view of paleontologist Dana Daring.

1   Deep in the heart of my museum laboratory, I work with bones. Big bones. Old bones. Dinosaur bones.

2   It's too big a job for one person. My team and I work for months or even years on just one case.

3   Our job begins when a crate of fossilized dinosaur bones arrives at the museum. **1**

4   Scientists in the field have found these bones. Now it's up to us to figure out how they fit together to make a dinosaur skeleton.

5   First we dig the bones out of the rocks and clean them off. We use power saws and electric drills, and hammers and chisels. We use special chemicals that melt the rock without hurting the bones. We don't stop until every bone is clean. **2**

6   We study the bones as we work. We try to figure out how big the dinosaur was, how it moved, and what it ate.

7   Next we try to fit the bones together in a complete skeleton. We use a metal frame to support the bones. Wire and pieces of metal hold the skeleton in place. If any bones are missing, we make new ones out of plastic or fiberglass. **3**

8   Finally, our dinosaur skeleton is complete, and I, Dana Daring, am happy. Nobody has ever seen a real, live dinosaur. They all died millions of years ago. But thanks to skeletons like this one, everyone can enjoy learning about my favorite creatures—dinosaurs! **4**

3. *I need to reread this paragraph more slowly so I can better visualize how they fit the bones together.* (Use fix-up monitoring strategies)

4. *Turn and talk to a partner. Tell what the author is describing. What is the purpose of the article?* (Summarize)

Extend Thinking Questions

Pose one or more questions to engage students more deeply with the text.

• *Even though dinosaurs don't live anymore, how do we know what they might have looked like?*

• *What do you think paleontologists look at in order to figure out how a dinosaur moved? What a dinosaur ate?*

iELD Paraphrase to Support Comprehension

After paragraph 4: *I work with other people. We could work for years on one project. We figure out how dinosaur bones fit together.*

After paragraph 5: *We use tools to get bones out of rocks. We try not to damage the bones. We clean the bones.*

After paragraph 7: *We support the bones as we try to fit them together. To do that, we use metal and wires. Missing bones can be made out of other materials.*

Unit 7

RI.2.1, RI.2.4, RI.2.6, L.2.2c, L.2.4c, RF.2.3d

Objective

• Model fix-up monitoring strategies

Set the Stage

Introduce the Text *Today I'm going to read aloud a story about a family visiting a museum. The kids learn about mummies when they stop in the Egyptian room.*

Engage Thinking *What do you know about mummies? Turn to a partner to share your thoughts.*

Engage with the Text

Read aloud the text at a fluent, expressive pace. Use the suggested prompts to model your thinking, clarify events, and elicit student interaction.

1. *The Egyptians' times are so different that I had a hard time following what I read. I will reread the paragraph, stopping after each sentence to make sure I understand.* (Use fix-up monitoring strategies)

2. *The word "himself" is a reflexive pronoun. That is when a word ends with -self or -selves. In this case, it refers to the pronoun "He" at the beginning of the sentence.* (Use reflexive pronouns)

Next Stop, Mummies!

1   Raj looked up from his museum guide. "Next stop, mummies!" he said as he led his parents and little brother, Sanjay, into the Egyptian room.

2   "Wait, this is a museum," replied Sanjay. "I thought museums only had real things, not fake stuff like werewolves and zombies and mummies."

3   "Mummies are real," said Dad. "They just didn't get up and walk around and scare people like they did in the movies."

4   "Yeah," said Raj. "A mummy is a real human body, or even an animal, that has gone through a process called mummification."

5   "What does that mean?" asked Sanjay. He looked at one of the mummies behind the glass case. It was wrapped in strips of cloth, just like ones he had seen in movies. He expected it to jump out at him and chase him through the museum. He backed up a couple feet and peeked into the next mummy case.

6   "Well, back in Egyptian times," said Mom, "people believed that they would journey to another world after they died. They thought that if they could keep their bodies in a special condition, then they could use it in their journey to the afterlife. Making the body into a mummy was the special process they had to go through. Then the mummy was put into a stone coffin for its journey." **1**

7   "They look terrible," said Sanjay. "Really creepy."

8   Raj read out loud from one of the signs on the wall. "The process of mummification took about seventy days," he said. "It cost a lot of money, too. That meant that only the rich could become mummies."

9   Sanjay was amazed at what he saw. He began reading some of the signs himself after a while. **2** "Eww," he said as he read the words aloud to his family. "It says here that the person's insides were taken out and only the heart was left for the journey. They put something in the body to dry it out, and then later put in sawdust."

10 "I wonder what it would be like to live back then," said Raj as he looked closely at mummy. They all felt that looking at the mummies was like looking straight back in time. **3**

11 "What do you think?" asked Dad. "Did we all learn something new and interesting at the museum today?"

12 Sanjay nodded his head. "That's for sure," he replied. **4**

3. *"Looking straight back in time" is an informal phrase. It means that by looking at something old, you are seeing the way things used to be.* (Compare formal and informal English)

4. *Turn and talk to a partner. Retell this story with the important facts and details. Be sure to use complete sentences and speak clearly.* (Summarize)

Extend Thinking Questions

Pose one or more questions to engage students more deeply with the text.

• *What is mummification?*

• *Just by looking at an Egyptian mummy, what could you probably say about the person from the past?*

iELD Paraphrase to Support Comprehension

After paragraph 5: *A family visits a museum. One of the children learns that a mummy is a body that was wrapped in cloth strips after it died.*

After paragraph 6: *Egyptians believed that they needed to keep their bodies in good condition after death. They thought they would journey to another world with their left-behind bodies. Putting a mummy in a coffin would keep the body safe.*

After paragraph 9: *Making a body into a mummy took about seventy days. The dead person's insides were taken out. The heart remained in the body, though. Only rich people could afford to become a mummy.*

CCSS
RI.2.1, RI.2.4, L.2.1c, L.2.3a, SL.2.4

Unit 7

Objective

• Model fix-up monitoring strategies

Set the Stage

Introduce the Text *Today I'm going to read aloud an informational text all about dinosaur poop and how it is studied.*

Engage Thinking *What do you think dinosaur poop has in it? Turn to a partner to share your prediction.*

Engage with the Text

Read aloud the text at a fluent, expressive pace. Use the suggested prompts to model your thinking, clarify events, and elicit student interaction.

1. *The word "loaf" is an irregular singular noun. It is only one loaf, but more than one loaf would be "loaves." You can't just add "s" to "loaf" for it to be plural. That's why it's irregular.* (Form irregular plural nouns)

2. *There are so many examples of what scientists can find in coprolites that I got lost. I think I need to read this paragraph again and envision each example after I read it.* (Use fix-up monitoring strategies)

The Scoop on Dino Poop

by Mary Meinking

1   What's as big as a loaf of bread, weighs as much as a frozen turkey, and tells us what dinosaurs ate? **1** Give up? It's a fossil of dinosaur poop, also known as a coprolite. The scoop on dino poop is finally flushed out!

2   Coprolites don't smell like poop after millions of years, because they've turned to stone. Their shape varies from small pellets to long logs, from curly spirals to flat pancakes. They also vary in color.

3   By studying coprolites, scientists have discovered what dinosaurs ate. Meat-eating dinosaurs' coprolites contain bone fragments, teeth, fish scales, or snail shells. And plant-eating dinosaurs' coprolites contain shredded wood, stems, leaves, flowers, or seeds. **2**

4   A world-record coprolite was found in Saskatchewan, Canada. **3** It's 17 inches long and 6 inches around. The coprolite contained the crushed bones of an unfortunate herbivore. The poop came from the largest carnivore in the area, a Tyrannosaurus rex.

5   This coprolite tells us not only what T. rex ate but how it ate. Previously, scientists believed that T. rex swallowed large chunks of meat and bones without chewing. But after examining the coprolite, they now realize that T. rex crushed mouthfuls of bones as it chewed. Bone fragments passed through the dinosaur's intestines in its poop.

6   Dr. Karen Chin is one of the scientists studying this giant T. rex coprolite. In fact, Dr. Chin is the world's leading paleoscatologist—a scientist who studies fossilized poop. To find out what's inside a coprolite, it is cut open, x-rayed, smashed, or sliced into superthin slices. The slices are studied under a powerful microscope. Dr. Chin is never sure what "jewel" she might find inside each coprolite. Who would have guessed that lumpy rocks could reveal such important information? Paleontologists, that's who. **4**

A coprolite of a carnivorous dinosaur

3. *Saskatchewan, Canada, is a geographic name found in the world, so you would capitalize both the province (Saskatchewan) and country (Canada).* (Capitalize geographic names)

4. *Turn and talk to a partner. Ask each other any questions you still have about this article and the other partner can try to answer it.* (Ask questions)

Extend Thinking Questions

Pose one or more questions to engage students more deeply with the text.

• *What do you think turns poop to stone after millions of years?*

• *What can paleoscatologists learn from studying dinosaur poop?*

iELD Paraphrase to Support Comprehension

After paragraph 3: *A piece of dinosaur poop is called a coprolite. Coprolites are hard. They vary in size and shape and color. What is found inside tells scientists what the animal ate.*

After paragraph 6: *A coprolite also tells a scientist how the dinosaur ate. Scientists have found that T. rex crushed bones as it ate. This shows us that they actually chewed their food. For study, coprolites are cut open, x-rayed, crushed, or sliced. Then they are looked at with a microscope.*

Unit 7

CCSS
RI.2.1, RI.2.4, L.2.1b, L.2.2a, SL.2.1c

Objective

• Model fix-up monitoring strategies

Set the Stage

Introduce the Text *Today I'm going to read aloud a story about a conversation that a mother has with her daughter. They had just stopped to see the ancient Pueblo people's homes built into the side of cliffs 900 years ago.*

Engage Thinking *What do you think the ancient Pueblo people used to build their homes in the cliffs? Turn to a partner to share your prediction.*

Engage with the Text

Read aloud the text at a fluent, expressive pace. Use the suggested prompts to model your thinking, clarify events, and elicit student interaction.

1. *The words "had" and "we" each have one syllable. However, one uses a short vowel and the other uses a long vowel. The "e" in "we" is a long vowel because of the sound it makes, and the "a" in "had" has a short vowel sound.* (Distinguish long and short vowels)

2. *A "tribe" is a collective noun because it is a group that is made up of a collection of individuals. In this case, the tribe was made up of Pueblo people.* (Use collective nouns)

Homes in the Cliffs

1   Rosa had been looking out the window at the wide-open sky for hours. "Are we there yet?" she asked. **1**

2   "Just about," said Mama. Rosa was surprised that they were finally almost there. They were on their way through Colorado and would be stopping to see the homes of ancient Pueblo tribes in an area called Mesa Verde. The homes were built nearly 900 years ago, right into the side of the cliffs. "What if you had a little bit of Pueblo in you, Rosa?" Mama asked. **2**

3   "Do you think I do?" said Rosa.

4   "Who knows," added Mama. "Maybe our own family members lived in these rocky homes in the cliffs 900 years ago."

5   When they arrived at the cliff dwellings, Rosa could not believe her eyes. It looked like a city built into the rock.

6   "Wow!" she said. "How did they build these amazing homes?"

7   "These are pueblo homes. The clay comes from the earth, and they were built right into the rocks. Some of these dwellings were like city buildings with more than 150 rooms." said Mama.

8   "That one has a ladder," Rosa pointed. "Why did they live so high above the ground?"

9   "Well, there are still things we don't know about the ancient Pueblo and how they lived," said Mama. "But they may have lived high in the rocks to stay safe." she continued.

10 "Yeah, I guess so. That makes sense," said Rosa. "But where did the people go?"

11 "Well," said Mama. "We think they were farmers who used these hills with the flat tops, called mesas, to do their farming. Then they started to leave the area when they couldn't farm here anymore. They moved south. They settled in the areas that are now Arizona and New Mexico." **3**

12 "We live in New Mexico!" said Rosa. "So, maybe we are related to some of the people who lived here."

13 "That's right, my little Pueblo child," said Mama.

14 "I can't believe these houses have just been sitting here for so long. They didn't fall apart. No one took them over," said Rosa.

15 "Well, it does help that this is a national park. The land is protected. We can visit them and study them to learn more about the past," said Mama.

16 "Do you think our house will last 900 years like these did?" asked Rosa.

17 Mama laughed. "There's no way," she replied, gazing up at the cliff dwellings. **4**

3. *I think I need to read this paragraph once more. I could summarize it to check my understanding. The people who lived in the cliffs were farmers. They used the mesas for farming. When they couldn't farm there anymore, they moved south to places such as Arizona and New Mexico.* (Use fix-up monitoring strategies)

4. *Turn and talk to a partner. Mama tells Rosa that there is no way that their house will last 900 years. Why might she think that?* (Make inferences/ predictions)

Extend Thinking Questions

Pose one or more questions to engage students more deeply with the text.

• *Mama said the Pueblo tribes might have lived high in the rocks to stay safe. But from what, do you think?*

• *What can we learn from the Pueblo tribes' homes in the cliffs?*

iELD Paraphrase to Support Comprehension

After paragraph 9: *Pueblo people lived about 900 years ago. They used clay to build their homes in the side of rocky cliffs. Some homes look like buildings in a city. The Pueblo tribes stayed safe high in the rocks.*

After paragraph 15: *The Pueblo people were farmers who used the flat-top hills to farm. They later moved south when they couldn't farm there anymore. The area became a national park, so the homes stayed just as they were built. Today, people can study them to learn about the past.*

CCSS
RL.2.1, RF.2.3a, L.2.1a, SL.2.1b

Unit 7

Objectives

- Model asking questions
- Model determining text importance
- Model summarizing/synthesizing

Set the Stage

Introduce the Text *Today I'm going to read aloud two poems. One is titled "The Wind," and the other is titled "Spring."*

Engage Thinking *What do you think will be the same about these poems? Turn to a partner to share your prediction.*

Engage with the Text

Read aloud the text at a fluent, expressive pace. Use the suggested prompts to model your thinking, clarify events, and elicit student interaction.

1. *I wonder what "trembling" means. What does it mean to be "trembling"? Use complete sentences to answer the question.* (Ask questions)

2. *"Neither you nor I" have seen the wind, as stated in this stanza of the poem. In the first stanza, "Neither I nor you" have seen the wind. Have students ask each other questions as to whether these words make sense and what they mean. Use complete sentences to answer the questions.* (Ask questions)

The Wind

by Christina Rossetti

Who has seen the wind?

Neither I nor you.

But when the leaves hang trembling,

The wind is passing through.

5   Who has seen the wind?

Neither you nor I.

But when the trees bow down their heads,

The wind is passing by.

Spring

by Anonymous

When the spring arrives,

when the daffodils bloom,

I hear the quiet winds.

I sit under a tree,

5   and I fall asleep. **4**

3. *This poem expresses that you can't actually see wind. But you can see the effects of the wind. You can just look at trees to know when there is wind.* (Determine text importance)

4. *Turn and talk to a partner. Summarize what is important in each poem.* (Summarize)

Extend Thinking Questions

Pose one or more questions to engage students more deeply with the text.

• *Trees don't actually have heads that bow. What does the author mean by "heads"?*

• *The author of "Spring" falls asleep. Why?*

iELD Paraphrase to Support Comprehension

After poem 1: *Nobody has seen the wind. But you know it is there when leaves and tree branches move.*

After poem 2: *In the spring, flowers bloom. There are soft breezes. The author falls asleep under a tree.*

Unit 8

CCSS
RL.2.1, RL.2.4, RI.2.2, RI.2.6, L.2.1f

Ten Thousand Buffalo on Our Roof

by Cynthia Light Brown

1   Hot, hot, hot. The sun felt like fire on my skin. My friend, the blue-tail lizard, usually likes to bake in the sun out by our tomato garden. But she had already scuttled into the shade. I scuttled into the shade, too. It was too hot for anyone!

2   It had been forever since it had rained, and the grass was hard and scratchy. Mom said the rains were late this year. I went into our house to find a cool spot, but the house felt like an oven. I imagined that I was a chocolate chip cookie. I oozed onto the floor and lay there, baking. **❶**

3   Just about when I figured I was a burned-up chocolate chip cookie, hard enough to break your teeth, I heard a soft ping. And a few seconds later, another ping. Then another, and another. The pings got louder and sharper. The sounds were coming from the roof, but it wasn't rain—it sounded like someone banging a spoon on a table.

4   "Mom!" I called out. "What's that noise?"

5   "Come see." She pointed outside.

6   I looked out the window. It looked like there was snow coming down. But this was July. It doesn't snow in July.

7   The pings had turned into a great roaring sound. Now it sounded like ten thousand buffalo were stampeding on our roof. My little brother and I jumped from sofa to chair and back again, whooping and hollering.

8   "Is it snowing?" I shouted. "Is it magic?"

9   "No," Mom hollered back. "It's not snow. It's hail."

10 The ground was turning white with little balls of ice, about as big as a nickel. It kept coming and coming and coming. **3**

11 After a while the sound of the charging buffalo slowed down to just a few pings, and then all of a sudden the hail stopped. My brother and I ran outside, barefoot.

12 We scooped up handfuls of the hail and ate them and threw them in the air. I shivered. The air was so cold I had to run back to get a sweater and shoes. In July!

13 I hope the blue-tail lizard found a safe place to hide during the hailstorm. Mom said animals are smart that way, so the lizard is probably OK. The tomato plants didn't make it, though; there's just a bunch of little stumps. And most of the leaves are gone from our trees. But it was worth it to have winter in July. **4**

4. *This story describes what it's like to experience a hailstorm in the middle of a hot summer. A change in nature can seem to come suddenly and completely transform the environment.* (Determine text importance)

Extend Thinking Questions

Pose one or more questions to engage students more deeply with the text.

• *What was the narrator's reaction to hail?*

• *Have you ever seen a change in the weather during the day? What happened, and how did you react?*

iELD Paraphrase to Support Comprehension

After paragraph 2: *It was very hot one day. It had been a really long time since it had rained. Inside the house was really hot too. The narrator pretends to be a cookie that was baking in the oven.*

After paragraph 11: *Small balls of hail started to fall. They made soft sounds on the roof. Then the sounds got louder. It started to sound like a lot of buffalo on the roof. The characters were so excited about the change in weather.*

After paragraph 13: *The ground became covered with hail. A piece of hail is a ball of ice about the size of a nickel. The sounds on the roof stopped just as quickly as they had come. My brother and I ran outside to play with the fallen hail. The hail had fallen hard and heavy. It destroyed the tomato plants. It even took leaves off of the trees.*

CCSS
RL.2.1, RL.2.2, RL.2.6, L.2.5a

Unit 8

Objectives

- Model asking questions
- Model determining text importance
- Model summarizing/synthesizing

Set the Stage

Introduce the Text *Today I'm going to read aloud an informational article that explains what makes wind.*

Engage Thinking *What do you think causes wind? Turn to a partner to share your prediction.*

Engage with the Text

Read aloud the text at a fluent, expressive pace. Use the suggested prompts to model your thinking, clarify events, and elicit student interaction.

1. *In "knocks down" you hear the /n/ sound in both words. The "k" in "kn" is silent, so it makes the same sound as "n" by itself.* (Generalize spelling patterns)

2. *Have students ask each other questions about how the sun makes outside air move. Use complete sentences to answer the question.* (Summarize/Ask questions)

3. *Turn and talk to a partner. Ask each other why some places are windier than other places. Use complete sentences to answer the question.* (Ask questions)

What Makes Wind?

1   Wind is moving air. It can move so gently that you barely feel it. Or it can blow so hard that it knocks down trees. **1**

2   You can make air move. Hold your hand in front of your mouth and blow. Can you feel air pushing against your hand?

3   But what makes the air outside move?

4   The sun!

5   Heat from the sun warms Earth's surface, which then warms the air above it. Warm air is lighter than cold air, so the warmed air floats up to the sky. As the warm air rises, cooler, heavier air rushes in to take its place. All that moving air is wind! **2**

6   You might have noticed that some places are windier than others. Why? One reason is that the sun doesn't heat places equally. **3**

7   Have you ever walked barefoot on a sandy beach on a sunny summer day? The sand can get so hot it burns your feet, while the ocean stays nice and cool.

8   Sand warms up faster than water. And the air above it warms up faster than the air above water. As the warm air over the beach rises, cooler winds blow in from the sea. That's why you can almost always feel a breeze on the beach. **4**

4. *Wind occurs naturally because of the sun. Heat from the sun warms the surface of Earth. This also warms the air closest to Earth. Cool air is heavier than warm air, so the cool air sinks to take the place of lighter warm air that floats up. The movement of the air creates wind.* (Determine text importance)

Extend Thinking Questions

Pose one or more questions to engage students more deeply with the text.

• *What are some times you have felt a lot of wind?*

• *If you know you are going to feel constant, cold wind, how might you dress?*

iELD Paraphrase to Support Comprehension

After paragraph 5: *Wind is the movement of air. Heat from the sun warms Earth. The air closest to the ground warms up. The colder the air, the heavier it is. So cold air sinks down, and warm air rises. Wind is caused by air trading places.*

After paragraph 8: *It takes water longer to warm up than it takes sand. At a beach, the air above the ocean water is cooler than above the sand. As warm air rises above the sand, cool air from the ocean rushes to take its place. That is why a beach usually has wind.*

Unit 8

CCSS
RI.2.1, RI.2.2, RI.2.4, RI.2.6, L.2.2d

Objectives

• Model asking questions

• Model determining text importance

• Model summarizing/synthesizing

Set the Stage

Introduce the Text *Today I'm going to read aloud two poems written by different authors. One is titled "Catching Snowflakes" and the other is titled "Snow Birds."*

Engage Thinking *How do you think the author catches snowflakes? Turn to a partner to share your prediction.*

Engage with the Text

Read aloud the text at a fluent, expressive pace. Use the suggested prompts to model your thinking, clarify events, and elicit student interaction.

1. *A regular verb ends in -ed when its conjugation is in the past tense. Each line so far in the poem uses irregular verbs, which means they are not regular. The present tense verbs in the poem are "fall," "catch," "ride," and "blows." In past tense, they are "fell," "caught," "rode," and "blew."* (Form past tense of irregular verbs)

2. *Turn and talk to a partner. Summarize the ways the child in the poem catches snowflakes. Based on this, ask each other to identify another way the child could catch snowflakes.* (Summarize/Synthesize)

3. *How does a bird leave a trail? Where do the little stars come from? Are the stars in the snow or in the air?* (Ask questions)

Catching Snowflakes

by Bonnie Widerman

When snowflakes fall from high above,

I try to catch them in my glove,

And when they ride on wind that blows,

I sometimes catch them on my nose.

5 But when each snowflake's gently hung

On drifting air, I use my tongue.

Snow Birds

by Charles Ghigna

We scatter seeds upon the snow

and watch the snow birds eat.

They leave a trail of little stars

beneath their tiny feet.

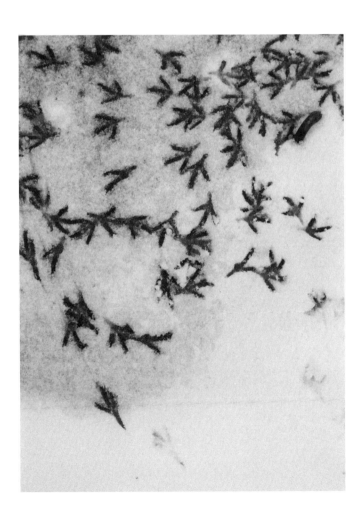

4. *The two poems describe peaceful events in the nature of winter. The first poem's author describes a few ways that she "catches" snowflakes as they fall. "Snow Birds" is about feeding birds some seeds and watching them eat. Star-shaped footprints are left behind on the snow.* (Determine text importance)

Extend Thinking Questions

Pose one or more questions to engage students more deeply with the text.

- *Have you ever tried to catch snowflakes? Does the way that you catch them depend on how they are falling?*

- *Why would the author of "Snow Birds" use "stars" to describe the trail that the birds leave?*

iELD Paraphrase to Support Comprehension

After poem 1: *Sometimes snowflakes fall from the sky onto my glove. Sometimes wind causes snowflakes to fly onto my face. Sometimes I can catch snowflakes with my tongue.*

After poem 2: *Birds eat the seeds on the snow that we give them. They leave pointy little footprints in the snow.*

Unit 8

CCSS
RL.2.1, RL.2.2, RL.2.6, L.2.1d

Objectives

• Model asking questions

• Model determining text importance

• Model summarizing/synthesizing

Set the Stage

Introduce the Text *Today I'm going to read aloud a factual article about the importance of water. It explains the effects of a drought, which is a time without water.*

Engage Thinking *What is one problem caused by a drought? Turn to a partner to share your thoughts.*

Engage with the Text

Read aloud the text at a fluent, expressive pace. Use the suggested prompts to model your thinking, clarify events, and elicit student interaction.

1. *Why does water likely have something to do with weather? Does it have to do with how water goes in a circle from clouds to land and ocean (also known as the water cycle)? If there is not enough water in an area, what kinds of problems will that cause?* (Ask questions)

2. *The word "wildfire" is a compound word, which means it is made of two individual words: "wild" and "fire." It literally means it is a fire in the wild; it is a fire in nature that could not be controlled.* (Determine word meaning)

Where's the Water?

1   What is the weather like today? Is it rainy, snowy, cloudy? No matter what the weather, water is likely to have something to do with it. But what happens when there is not enough water in an area? It rains or snows in one area and not another because water does not fall on Earth's surface evenly. Some areas do not get rainfall for a long time. A drought is a period of time when little or no rain falls on an area.

2   A drought can cause problems in a community. First, plants cannot get enough water to grow and stay alive. This causes problems for the animals that rely on those plants for food or shelter. **1**

3   Droughts cause problems for people, too. If a drought lasts a long time, there may not be enough water for everyone to use. A city or town may then ask people to use less water in order to help save, or conserve, the water supply. That may mean not watering your lawn or garden. Farmers may have to find other ways to feed their crops. During a serious drought, people may be asked to take shorter showers or to use less water in their everyday lives. Businesses may have to change the way they run so that they can use less water, too.

4   Droughts can even cause wildfires to start more easily in an area. **2** If the bushes, grasses, and trees are very dry, then they can start on fire easily. Lightning can cause a wildfire. Wind can make the fire spread.

5   While droughts can cause these problems, they are also a normal part of nature. Many droughts do not last long. Once it rains, water supplies return to normal.

6   Even during times when water supplies are normal, it is a good idea to not waste water. Always turn off the faucet when you are brushing your teeth. Don't leave the sprinkler on longer than needed. Any steps you take to save water may help your community if a drought does come your way. **3** **4**

3. *This article has described plenty of problems that can occur when there is not enough water in nature. We need to pay attention to when there are times of drought so that we can help prevent even more problems from it.* (Determine text importance)

4. *Turn and talk to a partner. Summarize what a drought is, the problems it can cause, and steps to take to save water.* (Summarize/Synthesize)

Extend Thinking Questions

Pose one or more questions to engage students more deeply with the text.

• *What kinds of problems could happen because of a drought?*

• *What are some things you can do to save water?*

iELD Paraphrase to Support Comprehension

After paragraph 1: *Water is usually involved with weather. When there is not enough water in an area for a long time, it is called a drought.*

After paragraph 4: *Many problems can occur from a drought. The time without water kills plants. Animals then have less food or shelter. Humans might take steps to save water in a drought. Fire can spread easily in dry areas with bushes, grasses, and trees.*

Unit 8

CCSS
RI.2.1, RI.2.2, RI.2.4, RI.2.6, L.2.4d

Objectives

- Model visualizing
- Model making inferences/predictions
- Model making connections

Set the Stage

Introduce the Text *A long time ago, there was no such thing as money. Today I'm going to read aloud an article that explains what it was like to barter, or trade, for what people needed.*

Engage Thinking *Why do you think money was invented? Turn to a partner to share your thoughts.*

Engage with the Text

Read aloud the text at a fluent, expressive pace. Use the suggested prompts to model your thinking, clarify events, and elicit student interaction.

1. *I can infer that trades are not always fair. In some cases, it depends on the quality of work done, and that level of quality changes from person to person. I predict that money is what replaced trade.* (Make inferences/predictions)

2. *I am visualizing a group of people wearing animal skins, walking out of their cave early one morning. They are carrying extra skins rolled up in a handmade bag, hoping to find someone along their journey who will trade for some fish to eat.* (Visualize)

Swap It!

1   Imagine there was no such thing as money. Instead of paying for a scrambled egg sandwich from the coffee shop down the block, you had to do something or trade something in exchange for the sandwich. What could you offer? You might say, "I'll sweep your floor for the sandwich." What if the floor is looking pretty clean already? What can you offer then? How about you offer to wash the coffee shop owner's car? That might work, but who is getting the better end of the bargain? Depends on how good the egg sandwich is, and how shiny and clean the car is after you wash it. **1**

2   Long ago, when people needed things, they bartered. If you have ever traded baseball cards with a friend, or swapped snacks with a classmate, then you have bartered. You got something that you needed or wanted in exchange for something else.

3   If we were to travel back in time to when life was very different, we would see what life looked like without money. People lived in caves. They ate whatever they could find. Clothing was made from animal skins. In a way, life was much more simple then. People used to travel in groups to search for food. They might run into another group of travelers and sometimes, the two groups might make a trade. Maybe animal skins for fish. Bartering made it possible for each group to get some of what the other group needed. **2**

4   Think of how life would be if every time you needed something, you had to make a swap: "I'll give you this sweater for that book." "I'll give you two pillows for one blanket." "I'll let you use my umbrella if you let me wear your rain boots." Every time you got something, you had to give up something.

5   Bartering had to have its share of problems. What if you wanted food, but you had nothing that the trader wanted? Or what if you needed medicine very badly and the only things you could offer were things you needed, such as cattle or water? If the person you were trading with knew that you needed something very badly, he might demand you give up a lot for it! It would be very difficult to make sure that all trades are fair to both people. **3**

6   Imagine also how hard life used to be back when people only made trades. You would have to travel on foot, with all your stuff, hoping to find what you needed, carrying all of your things to offer someone. You probably would be thinking, "There has to be a better way!" Well, there is. It's called money. Today we can find stores that carry the things we need, and we can know exactly what we must pay for them. What a relief! **4**

3. *Turn and talk to a partner. Describe the key ideas, or most important reasons, that explain the problems with bartering.* (Summarize)

4. *My prediction was correct. Money was created to replace trading goods and services. Money is a better substitute for people to get what they need. It is an easier solution to the problem, just as the last sentence states: "What a relief!"* (Make connections)

Extend Thinking Questions

Pose one or more questions to engage students more deeply with the text.

• *How did people get together with others in order to trade long ago?*

• *How is getting the goods and services you need today different from the ways of long ago?*

iELD Paraphrase to Support Comprehension

After paragraph 2: *Long ago, there was no money. People traded and bartered with each other to get what they needed.*

After paragraph 3: *People used to travel in search of shelter and food. They would carry their goods with them. They might trade with other travelers if they needed something different from what they had.*

After paragraph 6: *There were problems with bartering and trading. You would have to carry everything with you, and you might not find anyone who had what you needed. Money is easier. You can carry it to stores and find exactly what you need.*

Unit 9

CCSS
RI.2.1, RI.2.4, SL.2.2, L.2.3.a

Objectives

- Model visualizing

- Model making inferences/predictions

- Model making connections

Set the Stage

Introduce the Text *Today I'm going to read aloud a fictional article about a group of fifth graders who started a business called Little Lemons Lemonade Stand.*

Engage Thinking *What materials do you think the group needs to sell lemonade? Turn to a partner to share your prediction.*

Engage with the Text

Read aloud the text at a fluent, expressive pace. Use the suggested prompts to model your thinking, clarify events, and elicit student interaction.

1. *I can infer that a "glass of sunshine" is actually a "glass of lemonade." The writer is possibly making the lemonade sound very inviting and wonderful in order for the reader to want to buy some from the group.* (Make inferences/predictions)

2. *I can visualize four fifth graders: three girls and a boy, all in their yellow aprons. They are at a farmer's market, standing around their lemonade stand in between all of the other tents set up with other people's goods to sell. A few of the kids are smiling at passersby while the other one is busy filling a lemonade cup for a customer.* (Visualize)

3. *The tea choices they offer are sweetened and unsweetened. The prefix un- means "not," so it makes sense that they would offer sweetened tea and not-sweetened tea.* (Determine word meaning)

The Little Lemons

by Juan Peters

1 Summer is not the only time to enjoy a chilled glass of lemonade from the Little Lemons Lemonade Stand. The afternoon is the perfect time to buy a glass of sunshine ❶ from this young group of entrepreneurs. The Little Lemons usually set up shop in the park, but they are sometimes in other spots around town. They post their location on their website so that everyone knows just where to find the most delicious cup of lemonade in King's County.

2 The owners of Little Lemons are all in the fifth grade. There are three girls and one boy, and they are always busy thinking about how to improve their business. They believe they have an excellent product to offer. They make their lemonade slowly by hand, using the freshest lemons, spring water, ice, and sugar. They offer two sizes. There's thirsty, which is small, and crazy-mad thirsty, which is large.

3 The Little Lemons wear yellow aprons and always make a point to be polite and friendly to their customers. They often make quick decisions because one of the most important parts of their business is knowing where to set up their lemonade stand. They may be in the park on Mondays following a local baseball team, at the farmer's market on Tuesdays and Saturdays, and at the beach or by the pool on other days of the week. ❷

4 While lemonade is a tasty and delicious drink, not everyone loves it like the Little Lemons. That's why they offer an additional beverage. They brew sun tea and sell it with lots of ice and lemon wedges. They make two versions of tea, one sweetened and the other unsweetened. ❸ They do this because the Little Lemons know that consumers like to have choices.

5 The Little Lemon owners need some adult supervision when shopping for the lemons and paper cups, carrying the ice, and buying the materials they need to make signs. They have weekly business meetings to discuss ways to increase their profits. The Little Lemons spend about $50 a week on ingredients and supplies. Most weeks they more than triple that in profits.

6　On Sundays, the Little Lemons like to donate some of their money to a charity. The Little Lemons sell homemade brownies baked by their moms. The brownies are a special treat and people come from several towns to buy them.

7　During the months of January and February, the Little Lemons take a break from selling lemonade. Still, they meet every week to discuss ways to improve business. It is during this time that the Little Lemons may discuss expanding taking on another partner, or introducing another product. For now, they plan to keep things small. **4**

8　The Little Lemons say that when they reach the age of 18, they intend to take their business on the road. They want to operate Little Lemons Lemonade trucks. For now, profits are going into a college fund. The Little Lemons like to joke that "when life gives us lemons, we like to make lemonade."

4. *Turn and talk to a partner. Discuss why you think the Little Lemons take a break from selling lemonade in January and February. (Make connections)*

Extend Thinking Questions

Pose one or more questions to engage students more deeply with the text.

• *Why do you suppose the Little Lemons go to different places on different days to sell their goods?*

• *In what ways do the Little Lemons connect with their community?*

iELD Paraphrase to Support Comprehension

After paragraph 2: *A group of fifth graders owns the Little Lemons Lemonade Stand. They offer handmade lemonade in two different sizes. They tell people where to find them.*

After paragraph 6: *The Little Lemons sell other goods, too. They know that their customers make different choices. The group makes enough money to buy their materials and still have a lot left over. The Little Lemons like to give some money to a group that helps others, called a charity.*

After paragraph 8: *The Little Lemons do not sell in January and February. They still meet regularly to talk about how to make more money. That money goes toward saving for college.*

Unit 9

CCSS
RL.2.1, L.2.4b

Objectives

- Model visualizing
- Model making inferences/predictions
- Model making connections

Set the Stage

Introduce the Text *Today I'm going to read aloud an informational article about how much art is worth. A piece of art could sell for a small amount in the year it is finished, but years and years later, it could be sold for much more. This article will explain why.*

Engage Thinking *Why do you think art can be worth more to people many years later? Turn to a partner to share your prediction.*

Engage with the Text

Read aloud the text at a fluent, expressive pace. Use the suggested prompts to model your thinking, clarify events, and elicit student interaction.

1. *A famous artist made the painting that sold for more than $106 million. I predict that the artist's being well known has something to do with the price of the good.* (Make inferences/predictions)

2. *"Bought" is the past tense of the irregular verb "buy." Regular verbs end in -ed in past tense, but it would be incorrect to say "buyed."* (Use past tense of irregular verbs)

What Is Art Worth?

1   Have you ever made a painting and hung it on the wall, or on the refrigerator? Have you ever made a creature or object out of clay? Then you've made art! In the kid world, people don't think much about what art is worth. But in the adult world, art can be worth a lot of money!

2   One of the most expensive paintings ever sold cost more than $106 million. It was a painting by Spanish artist, Pablo Picasso. **1** The painting was sold in an auction in 2010. An auction is a kind of sale in which people who really want to own the painting tell how much they are willing to spend. This kind of sale makes the price of an item go higher and higher. People must decide if they are willing to pay more than the last person's offer. The person to make the highest offer pays the highest price and gets the painting.

3   Was Picasso's painting worth over $100 million when it was painted, back in the 1930s? No. So why are people willing to pay so much for it today? Picasso is famous around the world. People with a lot of money will pay more for famous art than for art made by artists who are not famous. They may hope to display the art. Then in years to come they may be able to sell it for even more than they bought it for. **2**

4   For example, if you make a painting, a friend may pay a dollar to buy it from you. Then in a few years, your friend may sell that painting for three dollars. If you become a famous artist one day, that painting will be worth a whole lot more. **3**

5   Most people do not make art because they want to become rich, though. People make art because they love to do it. If something is fun and enjoyable, then the time we spent on it is worth a lot to us. **4** Art is so valuable not only because it looks good. It is also valuable because it makes people happy.

A student makes a sculpture out of clay

3. *Turn and talk to a partner. Explain why your painting goes up in price over the years in this example.* (Make connections)

4. *To help me understand the sentence "If something is fun and enjoyable, then the time we spent on it is worth a lot to us," I envision playing at a beach. That time having fun could be the best part of the day and will be remembered for years to come. That time spent building sand castles and bobbing in the waves is worth a lot.* (Visualize)

Extend Thinking Questions

Pose one or more questions to engage students more deeply with the text.

• *How does an auction work?*

• *What does knowing people have to do with selling art?*

Paraphrase to Support Comprehension

After paragraph 2: *A piece of art at an auction is worth the most that someone is willing to pay for it.*

After paragraph 3: *Art could be worth even more over the years. Pablo Picasso was a famous painter. His paintings are worth a lot of money to some people because he was so well known.*

Unit 9

CCSS
RI.2.1, RI.2.4, L.2.1d

Objectives

- Model visualizing
- Model making inferences/predictions
- Model making connections

Set the Stage

Introduce the Text *Today I'm going to read aloud a narrative about making pottery. The narrator tells about all of the steps that his father takes in making his "different and wonderful" pieces of pottery, starting with the first sound in the morning and ending with the last sounds of the night.*

Engage Thinking. *What do you think the narrator hears first thing in the morning at a pottery maker's home? Turn to a partner to share your prediction.*

Engage with the Text

Read aloud the text at a fluent, expressive pace. Use the suggested prompts to model your thinking, clarify events, and elicit student interaction.

1. *I can infer that the "loud, smushy thwack" sound is from the clay that Daddy threw onto his potter's wheel.* (Make inferences/predictions)

2. *Adjectives describe nouns and pronouns. In this paragraph, "gooey" and "wet" are adjectives that describe the noun "clay." An adverb describes a verb, adjective, or other adverb. Many times, an adverb ends in -ly because it turns the root word into a way to describe how something is done. In the next sentence of the paragraph, "magically" is the adverb that describes the verb "grows." How does it grow? Magically.* (Use adjectives and adverbs)

The Potter's Wheel

by Alva Moore Joyner

1   The very first sound in our morning air is a loud, smushy *thwack*! **1** Then Daddy's potter's wheel begins to spin. We live at the foot of a great mountain, and our days move along, full of sound. The creek in our yard sings watery sounds, and little animals in the woods talk in their own way all day long. In our home, Daddy's wheel makes a gentle hum, and his hands make soft clucks as they move on and off the clay he has thrown onto his wheel.

2   When Daddy asks, I drip water onto the clay lump as it spins, making it wet. I watch the gooey, wet clay slip around and through his fingers. **2** Cupped in Daddy's hands, it magically grows and grows. Daddy is quiet when he works, but he smiles. He keeps the clay centered on his wheel as it turns, and he chooses a shape. Sometimes a tall, slim flower vase grows from the clay, guided upward by his strong fingers. Sometimes he slowly flattens the lump with the sides of his hand to form a plate. Sometimes nothing works, and Daddy says, "The clay isn't interested in 'becoming' today."

3   Then he laughs and pushes the sludge into a bag and saves it for tomorrow. He cleans his wheel, collects the pieces that became vases, plates, or bowls, and we go off to the shed. The shed is cool and quiet. Here, rows and rows of ivory-white bowls, cups, vases, and plates greet us on the shelves above Daddy's kiln. He adds his new work to the shelf. It looks damp and gray beside the old, but it will soon dry to match the ivory.

4   Then Daddy will paint it with glazes and fire it in his kiln. I love the days when a batch of work comes out of the kiln. After being baked at thousands of degrees for hours in the kiln, Daddy's work is allowed to cool, and then we see its colors for the first time. Blues and greens and sandy reds and vanillas cover cups and vases and platters and bowls that are all different and wonderful. **3**

5   The very first sound in our morning air is the loud, smushy thwack of clay on the potter's wheel, but the last sounds of our day are quieter. Daddy and I sit together before bedtime, listening to the mountain animals chattering softly as they bed down for the night. And sometimes we hear the potter's wheel spin, even when it's still. ④

3. *This paragraph helps me to visualize what it is like to see the finished pottery for the first time. After the pottery cools down from baking in a hot oven, the earthy colors show up, covering the clay cups, vases, plates, and bowls.* (Visualize)

4. *Turn and talk to a partner. Why does the narrator say they sometimes hear the potter's wheel spin, even when it's still?* (Make connections)

Extend Thinking Questions

Pose one or more questions to engage students more deeply with the text.

• *What pottery-making task does the narrator have?*

• *Do you think the narrator enjoys watching Daddy make pottery? Why or why not?*

iELD Paraphrase to Support Comprehension

After paragraph 1: *There are many sounds in the mountain where the narrator lives. The first thing he hears in the morning is Daddy throwing clay on his potter's wheel.*

After paragraph 4: *Daddy uses clay to shape his pottery on the spinning wheel. He is happy while he works. Sometimes, the clay doesn't take shape as he wants it to. So Daddy puts that clay back in a bag to try again later. He covers his pottery with a special coat of paint. Then he bakes them all in a very hot oven.*

After paragraph 5: *The day's sounds have calmed down by night. The potter's wheel may not be spinning, but the narrator can still remember the sound.*

CCSS
RL.2.1, RL.2.4, L.2.1e

Unit 9

The Gift

by Roderick Robinson

1   As he lay awake that night, Bebeto could hear his parents discussing his sister Ana's birthday. It was just two days away. Birthdays were always a lot of fun, even though there was no money for store-bought gifts. Nearly all of the toys he and his sister had were homemade. There was nothing wrong with that, he knew. Like many families in that part of Brazil, they were poor. This birthday would be different, though. Ana was older now, and he'd seen how her eyes lit up when she saw the new doll at Zulma's Presentes, a neighborhood store just down the road from their house. How he longed for her to have it!

2   An idea finally came to him just before he drifted off to sleep. After a quick breakfast the following morning, he placed a tin can and a section of a string in a burlap sack. Then he tied the sack to the handlebars of his bicycle and headed toward the outskirts of town. "Hello, young man," said the barber as Bebeto pedaled past the barbershop. "Time for a haircut today?"

3   "Not today, thanks. I've got to get a gift for my sister." ❷

4   Shortly after, he drove past a group of his friends playing soccer. "Come on over, Bebeto," they said. "You're just in time."

5   "Sorry guys. Not today," he said. The road grew steeper as he neared the outskirts of the town, and when he reached the hill country, he had to get off and push the bike the rest of the way. After a long trek, he reached his destination . . . the mango grove. There were already two other boys there, standing among some smaller trees and picking fruit from low branches. Bebeto grabbed his sack and set to work right away. The smaller trees had already been picked over pretty well, but he was able to find a half dozen mangoes before noon. After that, when the sun was high overhead, the hard work began. Nearly all of the taller trees held ripe mangoes, but they were well beyond reach. The other two boys took their fruit and went away. Bebeto bid them goodbye.

6   He used his pocket knife to cut a long piece of bamboo. Then he took the tin can from the sack, tied it to one end of the bamboo stick and walked over to the base of a mature mango tree. He stayed there, poking the tin can high up into the tree. His efforts were occasionally rewarded when a reddish-green mango plunked into the can. After a while his neck ached from looking upward, and his arms grew sore. He kept at it, though, and by late afternoon his sack was nearly full. On the way back to town, he began to worry that the other boys might have already sold or traded their mangoes to Zulma. **3** Maybe he was too late. He reached her store just before nightfall, as she was closing.

7   The following morning, Ana walked in and took a seat at the breakfast table. "Good morning, Birthday Girl," said her mother, pouring her a glass of passion fruit juice, and handing her a piece of sweet bread with lemon jelly on top. "I hear your brother has a special surprise for you today." **4**

8   Just then Bebeto came in, carrying a large bowl of mangos. He placed it on the table before Ana. "Happy birthday, Sis," he said.

9   "My favorite fruit. Thanks, Bebeto!" replied Ana. She reached for the bowl and picked up the top mango. Then her eyes widened, and her smile beamed even brighter. There, nestled among the fruit, was the new doll.

3. *Turn and talk to a partner. Remind each other who Zulma is, which was mentioned in the beginning. What do you think Bebeto is doing at her store?* (Make connections)

4. *I can picture Ana sitting at the table, the morning sunlight coming through the windows. She has a glass of orange liquid and bread with a yellow topping in front of her.* (Visualize)

Extend Thinking Questions

Pose one or more questions to engage students more deeply with the text.

• *Why had the smaller trees' mangoes already been picked?*

• *Who helped in Bebeto's plan to give his sister her gift? What did that person accept as payment?*

iELD Paraphrase to Support Comprehension

After paragraph 1: *Bebeto's sister, Ana, wanted a doll for her birthday. Bebeto didn't have money. But he really wanted to give her the doll!*

After paragraph 6: *Bebeto went to a place where mango trees grew. He tied a tin can to one end of a bamboo stick. He placed the can high in the tree and got the mango to fall in. He filled his bag with mangoes. Then, Bebeto went to the store.*

After paragraph 9: *Bebeto had traded some mangoes with the store owner. She let him trade for the doll. He hid the doll under the top mango in a bowl. His sister was happy to get her favorite fruit for her birthday. She was even happier and surprised to get the doll!*

Unit 9

CCSS
RL.2.1, RL.2.4, L.2.2c

Objectives

• Model asking questions

• Model determining text importance

• Model fix-up/monitoring strategies

Set the Stage

Introduce the Text *Today I'm going to read aloud an informational article that tells us how reusing trash is good for the earth. It also gives examples of several people or events around the world that focus on reusing items.*

Engage Thinking *What is one way you could reuse trash? Turn to a partner to share your thoughts.*

Engage with the Text

Read aloud the text at a fluent, expressive pace. Use the suggested prompts to model your thinking, clarify events, and elicit student interaction.

1. *How can people reuse trash? Could reusing my trash also save me money somehow?* (Ask questions)

2. *"Styrofoam" is a brand name, or the name of a product, so it is capitalized. In addition, "Texas" and "Baylor University" are capitalized because they are names of places you can visit.* (Capitalize product names)

3. *Under "They Make Sculptures!", the first paragraph describes how people in Kenya make elephant and giraffe sculptures from used flip-flops. The second paragraph describes how kids in Ohio used non-recyclable materials to make a big dinosaur model. So this section gives details about people reusing trash to make artwork.* (Determine text importance)

Turning Trash Into Art!

1 People reuse their garbage in some really fun ways.

2 Recycling is one way to help the planet. But there is another way that's even better—reusing! After all, trucks must deliver goods to be recycled at a factory. If you reuse items, trucks don't have to use as much fuel, and factories can save energy. **1**

3 Here are some ways people reuse their trash:

4 **They Make Clothes!**

5 Students at Baylor University in Texas held a unique fashion show. The show featured clothing made out of garbage! Models wore dresses made out of trash bags, used tablecloths, and Styrofoam cups. **2**

6 Many other people reuse trash to make a fashion statement. For example, Nancy Judd has worked to turn waste into fun and elegant styles.

7 **They Make Sculptures!**

8 In Kenya, hundreds of flip-flops wash up on the shore every day. Instead of throwing them out, local people collect the sandals and make them into colorful sculptures. They sell them as elephants and giraffes in Nairobi, the capital of the African country.

9 Kids in Portsmouth, Ohio, made an awesome sculpture too! They call it the Trashasaurus rex! "We used only non-recyclable materials," said fourth grader Brennan Overy who worked on the 15-foot dino. "It is really good to help the Earth by reusing your stuff," he told the *Portsmouth Daily Times.* **3**

10 **They Make Puppets!**

11 Second graders in Austintown, Ohio, made the news for their sustainable puppets! Each student got an old paper lunch bag. Then they used scissors, glue, and any garbage they wanted to make crazy garbage monsters!

12 Now it's time for you to have some fun! Make new things with old trash inside your home! And try not to buy anything new; besides scissors, glue, and tape, only garbage is allowed! ➍

4. *Turn and talk to a partner. Recall a paragraph that you had a hard time following because it was read too quickly. Ask each other questions to make sure you understand. (Use fix-up monitoring strategies)*

Extend Thinking Questions

Pose one or more questions to engage students more deeply with the text.

• *Why does the author say reusing is better than recycling?*

• *What are some ways you could make something with trash?*

iELD Paraphrase to Support Comprehension

After paragraph 5: *Reuse trash to save on costs and energy. There are many ways to reuse. One is to make clothes out of trash. Students at a school in Texas made clothes out of trash bags, tablecloths, and Styrofoam cups.*

After paragraph 9: *People in Kenya gather washed-up sandals from the ocean. They make them into models of elephants and giraffes. In Ohio, kids made a big dinosaur model out of trash that can't be recycled.*

After paragraph 11: *Kids in Ohio made puppets out of old paper lunch bags and other garbage.*

CCSS
RI.2.1, RI.2.4, RI.2.6, L.2.2a

Unit 10

Temika Makes Paper, Part 1

by Charman Simon

1   Temika's family was big on recycling paper. **①** Her dad flattened cardboard boxes and bundled newspapers. Her mom stacked magazines and catalogs. Her brother Tyler saved used computer paper instead of throwing it away.

2   "But where does all the paper go?" Temika asked. "I mean, after the recycling truck picks it up?"

3   "To make new paper," Tyler said. "We learned about it in science class. They take all the old paper and chop it up and mix it with water and make new paper." **②**

4   Temika kept making Grandma's birthday card. "I don't believe you," she said. "Paper is made from trees. We learned THAT in science class."

5   Mom spoke up before Tyler and Temika could start fighting. "You're both right," she said. "New paper is made of wood pulp made from ground-up trees. Recycled paper is made of pulp from ground-up old paper and cardboard. Recycled paper can be used to make lots of things—more paper, envelopes, cereal boxes, paper bags." **③**

6   "Making paper isn't that hard," Dad added. "We could make some right here at home. It's fun!"

7   Temika put down her scissors. Dad's projects were usually pretty messy. She looked sideways at Mom.

8   But Mom was smiling. "I used to send your dad love letters on homemade paper," she said, remembering. "I added rose petals and lavender buds."

9   "Gross," said Tyler.

10   Temika ignored him. "I want to make paper," she said. "Can I send Grandma a birthday card made of roses and lavender?"

11   "I don't see why not," Mom said. "Run and pick a few flowers while we get set up."

12 When Temika came in from the garden, Mom was stapling a piece of screen to an old picture frame. Dad was tapping the computer keyboard, and Tyler was tearing old sheets of computer paper into little pieces.

13 "There are lots of library books about making paper," Dad said. "And lots of websites, too. I think these directions look pretty good. Temika, you can help Tyler tear up paper. Try to use pieces that don't have too much printing on them. Too much ink will make your paper gray."

14 Mom took out the blender. "Fill about three-quarters full of water, right?" she asked.

15 "Yup," said Dad. "Then add paper scraps and blend."

16 Temika took a handful of torn-up paper. "But I don't want to make plain white paper," she said. "That's boring!"

17 "No problem," Mom said. "Throw in some of your construction paper scraps. They'll add just the right touch of color!" **4**

3. *There are some facts in this paragraph. I need to reread it slower so that I can really understand the difference between using trees or old paper and cardboard to make new paper. (Use fix-up monitoring strategies)*

4. *Turn and talk to a partner. What does the author mostly describe in Part 1 of the story? (Determine text importance)*

Extend Thinking Questions

Pose one or more questions to engage students more deeply with the text.

• *What can be made out of recycled paper?*

• *What information does Tyler give that Temika doesn't believe?*

iELD Paraphrase to Support Comprehension

After paragraph 5: *Paper and cardboard can be recycled. They are broken into smaller pieces. Then the pieces get mixed with water and turned into recycled paper. That paper can be used for many products.*

After paragraph 17: *Temika's family start to make paper. They use old sheets of computer paper and water. Mom is about to blend the two together when Temika says it will be too white. Mom tells her to add some construction paper for color.*

CCSS
RL.2.1, L.2.3a

Unit 10

Objectives

- Model asking questions
- Model determining text importance
- Model fix-up/monitoring strategies

Set the Stage

Introduce the Text *Today I'm going to read aloud Part 2 of "Temika Makes Paper." Temika will continue to learn how to make recycled paper.*

Engage Thinking *As the water and paper blend together, what food do you think Temika compares to the mixture? Turn to a partner to share your prediction.*

Engage with the Text

Read aloud the text at a fluent, expressive pace. Use the suggested prompts to model your thinking, clarify events, and elicit student interaction.

1. *I wonder how many pieces of paper the contents of the blender will make? If the mixture is like oatmeal, does that mean it's supposed to be blended until the old paper is the size of oats? Can you even tell the size of the old paper, or would it just look like dirty water?* (Ask questions)

2. *The prefix de- is used in the word "de-inker." One of the meanings of de- is "to remove" or "to reverse the action of." It makes sense in the context of the sentence because the de-inker removes the ink.* (Determine word meaning)

3. *Turn and talk to a partner. Read this paragraph again and summarize it to check your understanding.* (Use fix-up monitoring strategies)

Temika Makes Paper, Part 2

1   Temika put the paper in the blender and watched as the mixture turned mushy. "Like oatmeal," she said. **1**

2   "That's the pulp," Dad said. "In recycling plants, they put huge bales of old paper into a big vat of hot water called a pulper. The pulper chops up the paper, and the water helps turn the mix into pulp, just like our pulp here. Then they force the pulp through a screen to get rid of any staples or paper clips or other stuff that might be mixed in. And then they put the pulp through a machine called a de-inker to remove any ink. Finally they add bleach if they want the new paper to be really white." **2**

3   "And then," said Mom, "they mix the pulp in another big tub of clean water before they spray it on a huge screen and dry it into paper!"

4   "Is that what we're going to do?" Temika asked.

5   "Kind of," Mom said. "We don't need a de-inker or bleach or a sprayer. But we do need a big tub of water."

6   Dad set out the big plastic tub they used for bathing Bingo. He filled it with clean water, then watched Mom swish in a little white glue. "The glue makes the paper easier to write on," she explained. "Otherwise, the marker ink might soak right into the paper. Now, Temika—pour in the pulp and add your flowers!" **3**

7   The mushy pulp swirled into the clean water, little bits of flowers floating around in it. Mom showed Temika how to swish the framed piece of screen through the mush, and then to lift it straight up out of the tub.

8   "Now what?" asked Tyler.

9   Mom pointed to the thick pile of old newspapers she'd spread on the table. "Now we dry our paper," she said. "Can you put a clean dishtowel over these newspapers? It'll help absorb the water, and we won't get newsprint smears on our paper."

10 Carefully, Mom showed Temika how to flip the frame over on the clean towel. They pressed down on the screen with a sponge to soak up some of the water. Then they lifted the frame—and there on the towel was a square of pinkish paper, with bits of rose and lavender scattered across it.

11 "Here," said Mom. She handed Temika another dishtowel. "Press it down on your paper—that's right—and now use this rolling pin to squeeze out still more water. Good!"

12 Very carefully, Mom helped Temika lift off the top towel. Still more carefully, they peeled away Temika's paper from the bottom towel. "Now," said Mom, "we stick it on the window to finish drying. That's the fastest way to get a smooth piece of paper!" **4**

13 Temika grinned as she pressed her damp piece of paper to the window. "How long before I can write on it?" she asked.

14 "A couple of hours," Mom said. "Just enough time to clean up this mess and think of what you want to say to Grandma!"

4. *In the beginning of Part 2, Dad explained the pulp process of the recycling factory. Mom explained another easy process. But they still had to carefully follow directions.* (Determine text importance)

Extend Thinking Questions

Pose one or more questions to engage students more deeply with the text.

• *What does a recycling plant do to make paper white?*

• *What is the homemade process of making paper?*

iELD **Paraphrase to Support Comprehension**

After paragraph 3: *In a recycling factory, old paper goes into a tub of hot water. The container is called a pulper. The hot water breaks the paper down into pulp. The pulp then goes through a screen. Unwanted, bigger objects get separated from the pulp. A machine removes ink from the pulp of the old paper. Bleach whitens the paper. Pulp is then rinsed and sprayed onto a screen to dry.*

After paragraph 12: *Mom added glue to a tub of clean water. Temika mixed in the pulp and flowers. They screened out some of the pulp mixture. They flipped the screen upside-down onto a towel and soaked up some of the water with a sponge. They removed the screen and saw the new paper. Temika put a dry towel on the paper and rolled over it with a cylinder shape. The top towel came off, and they pulled the wet paper off the bottom towel. They stuck it on the window to dry.*

CCSS
RL.2.1, RL.2.6, L.2.4b

Unit 10

Objectives

- Model asking questions

- Model determining text importance

- Model fix-up monitoring strategies

Set the Stage

Introduce the Text *Today I'm going to read aloud a story told by a 5-year-old boy named Trevor. He talks about living by a river and keeping it clean.*

Engage Thinking *What do you think is Trevor's favorite job to do when his group cleans the river? Turn to a partner to share your prediction.*

Engage with the Text

Read aloud the text at a fluent, expressive pace. Use the suggested prompts to model your thinking, clarify events, and elicit student interaction.

1. *"Clean" is an adjective that describes the water being free of pollution. "Clean" can also describe something that is free from dirt and other unwanted things. For example, dishes, cars, and hands can be clean.* (Make connections)

2. *What is so important about looking for water bugs? Why do they need to catch them? Are the bugs bad for the water somehow? Are they trying to get rid of them?* (Ask questions)

3. *This paragraph is made of two long sentences. I need to read them again slowly and pause at each comma and period to make sure I understand what I just read.* (Use fix-up monitoring strategies)

Our Stream Team

by Rachel Young

1   Hi! My name is Trevor. I'm five years old, and I live in Missouri, near a river called the Jacks Fork. Before I was born, my grandpa Ted and grandma Pat decided they wanted to help keep the river clean. **1** So they started a club called Stream Team 713. I like our other name better—the Jacks Fork River Rats!

2   The River Rats make sure the water is clean and healthy for fish and people. And now I'm big enough to help take care of the river too. Come see!

3   Picking up trash is sort of like a treasure hunt. My friends and I find bottle caps, cans, candy wrappers, and all sorts of stuff. But there used to be even more garbage here.

4   In one weekend, my grandparents once picked up six tons of trash. That's as much as an elephant weighs! That garbage wasn't good for the river or the animals and plants that lived there.

5   So the River Rats taught people who were fishing or canoeing on the river to take trash with them rather than throwing it in the water. Now there's much less trash for us to pick up.

6   Here's all the garbage we found today. If we keep telling people not to trash the river, maybe one day we won't find any garbage here.

7   Now it's time for my favorite job—looking for water bugs! **2** The bugs like to burrow into the mud and rocks at the river bottom. So some big kids do a funny bug dance to stir up the rocks. My grandpa has a big net to catch the bugs as they float downriver.

8   Some bugs don't care how dirty the water is, but other bugs can only live here if the water's clean. If we find lots of bugs who need clean water, then we know the river is clean enough for fish and for us. **3**

9 Look at all the cool bugs we found! When we're done counting, we put them back in the water. We want there to be lots of bugs in the river, so the fish have something to eat.

10 We're done cleaning up and counting bugs. Now it's time for swimming! I love taking care of the Jack's Fork River. We help make sure it's a clean and safe place for me and my friends to play. **4**

4. *Turn and talk to a partner. Discuss the importance of water bugs for the river.* (Determine text importance)

Extend Thinking Questions

Pose one or more questions to engage students more deeply with the text.

• *What has Trevor found at the river that he calls garbage? What kind of garbage have you found around your home?*

• *What do the River Rats do to make their river like new? What can you do to make the land around your home like new?*

iELD Paraphrase to Support Comprehension

After paragraph 4: *The name of a river where Trevor lives is called Jacks Fork. His grandparents wanted to keep the river clean. They formed a group to do that. Trevor likes to call the group the River Rats. Trevor is now old enough to help clean. Trash in the river is bad for plants and animals, including people.*

After paragraph 9: *The River Rats told other people who use the river not to use it as their trash can. The River Rats count the water bugs that live in the river. The bugs like to live in clean water. If there are a lot of bugs, then the river is clean enough for people and fish. Also, the bugs are good for fish to eat.*

CCSS
RI.2.1, RI.2.4, RI.2.6, L.2.5a

Unit 10

Objectives

- Model asking questions

- Model determining text importance

- Model fix-up monitoring strategies

Set the Stage

Introduce the Text *Today I'm going to read aloud a story about a boy named Rico who goes to Nana's house after school. He is hungry, so he asks for a snack.*

Engage Thinking *What particular snack do you think Rico will ask for? Turn to a partner to share your prediction.*

Engage with the Text

Read aloud the text at a fluent, expressive pace. Use the suggested prompts to model your thinking, clarify events, and elicit student interaction.

1. *The word "dinnertime" is a compound word. That means it is made up of two individual words. In this case, they are "dinner" and "time." Together, the compound word means "time of dinner."* (Determine word meaning)

2. *The story says that bananas that are old, too ripe, and mushy are perfect. How could they possibly save the day? Does Nana expect Rico to eat one as his snack? Or does she have some other plan for the bananas?* (Ask questions)

Mushy Bananas

by Roderick Robinson

1   Rico hopped off the school bus and ran into Nana's house. "I'm here," he yelled as he dropped his book bag and jacket at the door until his mother could pick him up around dinnertime. **1**

2   Nana stuck her head out of the kitchen doorway. "Don't forget to take off your shoes!" she said as he settled in and rolled on the floor as her dog, Bear, licked his face.

3   "I'm hungry," said Rico in a serious tone as he stopped petting Bear. He wandered into the kitchen. "Do you have any bananas?"

4   Rico saw the dark, spotted bananas on the countertop. "Eww, Nana," he said. "It looks like you should have thrown those bananas away. They're getting rotten and mushy."

5   Nana walked over to the bananas. "Oh, they're perfect now. Would you like to see how these old, over-ripe, mushy bananas are going to save the day?" she asked. **2**

6   "Now this, I've got to see," said Rico. "What are you going to do with them?"

7   "We are going to make a banana bread with them," she replied. "Those bananas may look gross now, but my banana bread recipe calls for three of these over-ripe bananas. Not green, not yellow, but nearly brown!"

8   "Why should they be so brown?" asked Rico. "It seems like we shouldn't be eating bananas like that."

9   "Well, the bananas change over time," she said. "First, they are green, which means that they are not yet ripe. Then they turn yellow. That's when they are ripe and ready to eat. Then when they get brown, they are overripe and soft. That's when we use them in a recipe. They will mix well with the other ingredients: eggs, butter, flour, and sugar. When we bake the mixture in the oven, it changes from a wet batter to a solid cake. The soft bananas bake well." **3**

10 Rico scratched his head. "I didn't know your banana bread was made with old bananas. It's the best bread ever. Can we make one right now?"

11 "Sure," replied Nana. "But just remember that you have to wait to get your snack."

12 "Oh, I'll wait," replied Rico happily. "It will be worth it. Those old bananas will have a new life!"

3. *Turn and talk to a partner. Reread this paragraph, stopping after each sentence. Afterward, summarize how a banana changes over time.* (Use fix-up monitoring strategies)

4. *Even if bananas are not eaten in one form, there is still hope to use and enjoy them in another form.* (Determine text importance)

Extend Thinking Questions

Pose one or more questions to engage students more deeply with the text.

• *Why did Rico want to throw away the bananas on the countertop?*

• *What did Rico mean when he said the old bananas will have a new life? Can you think of other ways to give food new life?*

iELD Paraphrase to Support Comprehension

After paragraph 4: *Rico wanted to eat a banana as an after-school snack, but he saw that Nana only had dark, mushy ones.*

After paragraph 9: *Nana said the mushy bananas were perfect for what she was planning. She was waiting for them to ripen, or get older. Now she can use them to bake a banana bread.*

CCSS
RL.2.1, RL.2.6, L.2.4d

Unit 10

Grade 2 Passage Matrix

Unit	Unit Topic	Title	Author/Source
1	Government at Work	Jake and Jackie for President	J. McGillian
1	Government at Work	Government Is for Kids	Mike Weinstein
1	Government at Work	John Muir: A Friend of Nature	N/A
1	Government at Work	Let's Celebrate!	N/A
1	Government at Work	What Is a Jury?	N/A
2	Characters Facing Challenges	Hadley, the Helped-Along Walrus	Tim Bascom
2	Characters Facing Challenges	Princess Clarabelle	Elizabeth Passarelli
2	Characters Facing Challenges	The Giving Dog (Part 1)	Jamie McGillian
2	Characters Facing Challenges	The Giving Dog (Part 2)	Jamie McGillian
2	Characters Facing Challenges	Silly Things	Alison Acheson
3	Plants and Animals in Their Habitats	Worms to the Rescue	Joy Elizabeth Hancock
3	Plants and Animals in Their Habitats	In the Garden	Emily Dickinson
3	Plants and Animals in Their Habitats	Fly Away, Ladybug!	N/A
3	Plants and Animals in Their Habitats	Keeping Warm	N/A
3	Plants and Animals in Their Habitats	I, Mouse	Ruth Lercher Bornstein
4	Many Characters, Many Points of View	Dog Talk	Pat Trollinger
4	Many Characters, Many Points of View	Dad's Big News	N/A
4	Many Characters, Many Points of View	The Basket Weaver (Part 1)	Jacque Summer
4	Many Characters, Many Points of View	The Basket Weaver (Part 2)	Jacque Summer
4	Many Characters, Many Points of View	Good Sports	N/A
5	Solving Problems Through Technology	Are You Meant to Invent?	Karen Bradley Cain
5	Solving Problems Through Technology	The Wright Brothers Take Off	Mike Weinstein
5	Solving Problems Through Technology	Willy Wriggler's Wheels	Kathleen M. Muldoon
5	Solving Problems Through Technology	Texting: Yes or No?	N/A
5	Solving Problems Through Technology	The Traffic Signal: A Bright Idea from a Bright Inventor	N/A
6	Tales to Live By	A Man and His Precious Cow	N/A
6	Tales to Live By	Happy New Year!/Chinese New Year	Pat Sandifer Borum/Jacqueline Schiff
6	Tales to Live By	Brother Tiger and the Well, Part 1	William Kelly
6	Tales to Live By	Brother Tiger and the Well, Part 2	William Kelly
6	Tales to Live By	Sijo Poems	N/A
7	Investigating the Past	Long Gone	Jack Prelutsky
7	Investigating the Past	Dana Daring: Dino Detective	Dana Daring
7	Investigating the Past	Next Stop, Mummies!	N/A
7	Investigating the Past	The Scoop on Dino Poop	Mary Meinking
7	Investigating the Past	Homes in the Cliffs	N/A
8	Wind and Water Change Earth	The Wind/Spring	Christina Rossetti/Anonymous
8	Wind and Water Change Earth	Ten Thousand Buffalo on Our Roof	Cynthia Light Brown
8	Wind and Water Change Earth	What Makes Wind?	N/A
8	Wind and Water Change Earth	Catching Snowflakes/Snow Birds	Bonnie Widerman/Charles Ghigna
8	Wind and Water Change Earth	Where's the Water?	N/A
9	Buyers and Sellers	Swap It!	Jamie McGillian
9	Buyers and Sellers	The Little Lemons	Juan Peters
9	Buyers and Sellers	What Is Art Worth?	N/A
9	Buyers and Sellers	The Potter's Wheel	Alva Moore Joyner
9	Buyers and Sellers	The Gift	Roderick Robinson
10	States of Matter	Turning Trash Into Art!	N/A
10	States of Matter	Temika Makes Paper, Part 1	Charman Simon
10	States of Matter	Temika Makes Paper, Part 2	Charman Simon
10	States of Matter	Our Stream Team	Rachel Young
10	States of Matter	Mushy Bananas	Roderick Robinson

Lexile®	Text Type	Genre	CCSS-ELA	HSS	NGSS
590L	Literary	Realistic Fiction	RL.2.1, RL.2.3, RL.2.4, L.2.4c		
730L	Informational	Social Studies	RI.2.1, RI.2.4, L.2.4a, L.2.4b, SL.2.4	2.1.2	
790L	Informational	Social Studies	RI.2.1, RI.2.4, L.2.1d, L.2.2c, SL.2.3	2.3.2, 2.5	
870L	Informational	Social Studies/Letter	RI.2.1, RI.2.4, L.2.1b, L.2.4d, SL.2.2, SL.2.3	2.1.2	
790L	Informational	Social Studies	RI.2.1, RI.2.4, L.2.1a, L.2.2d, SL.2.6	2.3.2	
330L	Literary	Fiction	RL.2.1, RL.2.3, RL.2.4, L.2.5a, L.2.6		
750L	Literary	Realistic Fiction	RL.2.1, RL.2.3, L.2.4e, SL.2.3		
790L	Literary	Realistic Fiction	RL.2.1, RL.2.3, L.2.3a, L.2.4b, SL.2.2		
620L	Literary	Realistic Fiction	RL.2.1, RL.2.3, L.2.1e, L.2.2b		
540L	Literary	Realistic Fiction	RL.2.1, RL.2.3, L.2.1f, L.2.2a, SL.2.4		
740L	Informational	Science	RI.2.1, RI.2.6, L.2.1e, SL.2.3		2-LS4-1
NP	Literary	Rhythmic Poetry	RL.2.1, RL.2.4, RL.2.6, L.2.5b, SL.2.4		
1120L	Informational	Science	RI.2.1, RI.2.4, RI.2.6, L.2.4a, L.2.5a, SL.2.3		2-LS4-1
1000L	Informational	Science	RI.2.1, RI.2.4, RI.2.6, RI.2.8, L.2.1b, L.2.1e		2-LS4-1
1140L	Literary	Free Verse Poetry	RL.2.1, RL.2.4, L.2.2e, L.2.3a		
390L	Literary	Realistic Fiction	RL.2.1, RL.2.4, L.2.2c, L.2.1e		
610L	Literary	Realistic Fiction	RL.2.1, L.2.1d, L.2.2a, L.2.3a		
760L	Literary	Fable	RL.2.1, L.2.2d, L.2.4a, SL.2.2		
620L	Literary	Fable	RL.2.1, RF.2.3d, L.2.1f, L.2.4c, L.2.4d		
500L	Literary	Fiction	RL.2.1, RL.2.6, L.2.1b, L.2.4e		
880L	Informational	Science	RI.2.1, RI.2.2, L.2.2a, L.2.5a, RF.2.3f		K-2-ETS1-1
830L	Informational	Science	RI.2.1, RI.2.2, RI.2.4, L.2.1d, L.2.2c, L.2.4a, SL.2.1a	2.5	K-2 ETS1 1
690L	Literary	Fiction	RL.2.1, RF.2.3a, L.2.1e, L.2.2d, SL.2.2		
810L	Informational	Opinion	RI.2.1, RI.2.2, RI.2.4, L.2.1c, L.2.2b, L.2.6, SL.2.1a		K-2-ETS1-3
740L	Informational	Science	RI.2.1, RI.2.4, RI.2.6, L.2.1d, L.2.2a, L.2.4d	2.5	K-2-ETS1-1
570L	Literary	Folktale	RL.2.1, RL.2.2, RL.2.4, L.2.4a, L.2.5a		
NP	Literary	Free Verse/Rhythmic Poetry	RL.2.1, RL.2.4, L.2.1f, L.2.2c		
630L	Literary	Folktale	RL.2.1, L.2.2d, L.2.4c, SL.2.4		
670L	Literary	Folktale	RL.2.1, RL.2.2, L.2.1d, L.2.5b, SL.2.3		
NP	Literary	Rhythmic Poetry	RL.2.1, RL.2.4, L.2.2e, L.2.4b, L.2.4d		
NP	Literary	Rhythmic Poetry	RL.2.1, RL.2.4, RL.2.5, L.2.4e		
670L	Informational	Science	RI.2.1, RI.2.4, RI.2.6, L.2.2c, L.2.4c, RF.2.3d		K-2-ETS1-2
680L	Literary	Realistic Fiction	RI.2.1, RI.2.4, L.2.1c, L.2.3a, SL.2.4		
890L	Informational	Science	RI.2.1, RI.2.4, L.2.1b, L.2.2a, SL.2.1c		2-ESS1-1
590L	Literary	Realistic Fiction	RL.2.1, RF.2.3a, L.2.1a, SL.2.1b		
NP	Literary	Rhythmic/Free Verse Poetry	RL.2.1, RL.2.2, RL.2.6, L.2.1f		
540L	Literary	Realistic Fiction	RL.2.1, RL.2.2, RL.2.6, L.2.5a		
640L	Informational	Science	RI.2.1, RI.2.2, RI.2.4, RI.2.6, L.2.2d		2-ESS1-1
NP	Literary	Rhythmic Poetry	RL.2.1, RL.2.2, RL.2.6, L.2.1d		
790L	Informational	Science	RI.2.1, RI.2.2, RI.2.4, RI.2.6, L.2.4d		2-ESS2-3
730L	Informational	Social Studies	RI.2.1, RI.2.4, SL.2.2, L.2.3a	2.4.2	
1000L	Literary	Realistic Fiction	RL.2.1, L.2.4b	2.4.2, 2.4.3	
810L	Informational	Social Studies	RI.2.1, RI.2.4, L.2.1d	2.4.2	
1010L	Literary	Realistic Fiction	RL.2.1, RL.2.4, L.2.1e		2-PS1-2
780L	Literary	Realistic Fiction	RL.2.1, RL.2.4, L.2.2c	2.4.2	2-PS1-2
750L	Informational	Science	RI.2.1, RI.2.4, RI.2.6, L.2.2a		K-2-ETS1-2
530L	Literary	Realistic Fiction	RL.2.1, L.2.3a		2-PS1-2, K-2-ETS1-1
850L	Literary	Realistic Fiction	RL.2.1, RL.2.6, L.2.4b		2-PS1-2, K-2-ETS1-1
760L	Informational	Science	RI.2.1, RI.2.4, RI.2.6, L.2.5a		2-ESS2-3
590L	Literary	Realistic Fiction	RL.2.1, RL.2.6, L.2.4d		2-PS1-4

Notes:

Grade 2

Notes:

Notes: